Sri Vidya
Divine Radiance Within

Retreat Discourses
Penusila, November 6 - 11, 2002

Karunamayi
Bhagavati Sri Sri Sri Vijayeswari Devi

Sri Matrudevi Visvashanti Ashram Trust, Inc.
(SMVA Trust, Inc.)

Published under the auspices of:

SRI MATRUDEVI VISVASHANTI ASHRAM TRUST
Penusila Kshetram, Nellore Dt., Andhra Pradesh 524342, India.

KARUNAMAYI SHANTI DHAMA
14/5, 6th Cross, Ashok Nagar, Banashankari lst Stage,
Bangalore 560050, India.

SMVA TRUST, Inc.
14516 Rumfeldt, Austin, TX 78725, USA.

KARUNAMAYI VISWASHANTHI FOUNDATION
London, England, U.K.

1st Edition:	1000 copies
Reprinted 2009:	1000 copies

Printed by: McNaughton & Gunn, Inc.
Saline, Michigan 48176

Karunamayi Sri Sri Sri Vijayeswari Devi

ACKNOWLEDGEMENTS

Sri Vidya - Divine Radiance Within contains discourses given by our beloved Amma Karunamayi, Bhagavati Sri Sri Sri Vijayeswari Devi at Her Penusila Ashram during a retreat held in November 2002. These divine discourses would not have been made available to the world but for the devoted and conscientious effort of Smriti Dudley to record them.

Sincere thanks to all the transcribers, editors and formatters who have made this work possible.

TABLE OF CONTENTS

Foreword vii

Pronunciation Key x

Sri Vidya Retreat Discourses:

Welcome to Penusila 1

Sri Vidya is the Knowledge of Mother Divine . . . 7

Sri Vidya is the Highest Knowledge 9

Sri Vidya leads to Moksha 23

Sri Vidya: Practices and Qualifications 32

Inquiry into the Meaning of Truth 41

Sacred Khadga Mala Stotram: Hridaya Devi 55

Illumine the Inner Sky 62

Sri Vidya dispels the Darkness of Ignorance 74

Siro Devi: Divinity of the Sahasrara 78

Sri Khadga Mala - Waves of Effulgence 81

Power of the Bijakshara "Aim" 84

Sri Vidya is Open to All 92

Sikha Devi bestows Complete Inwardness 96

Blessings of Sikha Devi and Netra Devi 108

Kavacha Devi: The Shield of Protection. 122
Sri Lalita Sahasranama: Most Powerful Shastra . . . 128
The Five Shariras, Bodies 136
Sri Vidyam Shloka 142
Questions from Sadhakas 148
Benefits of Khadga Mala Stotra 154
Khadga Mala Prayer Shlokas 156
Universal Energies in the Khadga Mala 163
The Blessings of Sri Vidya 168

Appendix:

A Morning Outing with Amma 183

FOREWORD

What is *Sri Vidya?* The word *Sri* means light, treasure, majesty and beauty; it is also the name of Maha Lakshmi Devi, the luminous form of Divine Mother who bestows all prosperity—both worldly and spiritual—upon us. *Vidya* means knowledge. *Sri Vidya* is the priceless treasure of true knowledge of the highest Consciousness. It is also known as *Maha Vidya,* the greatest knowledge, *Atma Vidya,* knowledge of the soul, and *Moksha Vidya,* the knowledge that leads to liberation and eternal bliss. It is the supreme education, in which the answers to all questions are found. It is the knowledge of the light within each and every being, the formless Divine, which has also been envisioned since ancient times as the radiant, exquisite form of Divine Mother.

From the moment Sri Karunamayi first came to the United States in 1995, She has been lovingly but firmly urging us to meditate and attain the glorious experience of Self-Realization. Year by year, She has showered us with compassion and *mantras* and the most beautiful teachings from the ancient *vedic* tradition, while constantly encouraging us to meditate and discover the greatest treasure inside ourselves.

At the time of Amma's first visit, very few of us had heard of *Sri Lalita Sahasranama,* the thousand names of Divine Mother. With infinite tenderness, She talked to us about this beautiful and supremely powerful *stotram,* a hymn of praise extolling the glories of Mother Divine. Blessed by Amma's grace, thousands of devotees all over the world now chant the *Lalita Sahasranama* daily with faith and devotion.

Over the next few years, Amma introduced us to the *Sri Chakra,* the sublime geometric symbol of cosmic energy, the manifested universe and the individual self. She patiently taught us the *Sri Suktam* and the *Samputita Sri Suktam*, ancient hymns invoking the light and protection of Maha Lakshmi Devi. We learned to chant them, adding them to our daily spiritual practice not only for our own benefit, but for the benefit of all life. Little did we know that our beloved Mother was gradually initiating us into *Sri Vidya,* the most secret worship of the eternal, all-pervasive supreme Consciousness.

Then in November 2002, Sri Karunamayi chose *Sri Vidya* as the subject of a six-day silent meditation retreat for westerners. She offered this retreat at Her *ashram* in Penusila, a remote, forested area of South India, in whose beautiful mountains the *rishis* themselves long ago meditated on *Sri Vidya*.

This knowledge is so powerful that from time immemorial only the most dedicated and elevated spiritual seekers have been initiated into *Sri Vidya.* Over the centuries, and even more so today, few aspirants could make a firm lifelong commitment to the strict rules regarding its daily practice, and the gates of the magnificent mansion of *Sri Vidya* remained closed to ordinary human beings.

But Sri Karunamayi is the very embodiment of compassion. She sees only divinity and goodness in all Her children. She is our loving Mother who feels that each and every one of us, no matter what our shortcomings, is eligible to enter the glorious palace of this great *Atma Vidya*. "Everyone in the world is longing for *shanti,* peace," She tells us. "Amma is opening the doors of *Sri Vidya* for the whole world. You need only open your hearts and enter to attain the experience of peace and light."

Amma makes this rare knowledge accessible to today's aspirants by transmitting to us the inner essence of its teachings, impressing the point that this expression of Truth from the ancient tradition of India is the heritage of all people. She shows us how the *Sri Chakra,* the *Khadga Mala Stotram* and *Sri Lalita Sahasranama* guide us in unlocking the divine radiance within ourselves; in pursuing this inner path, we discover our connection to this glorious light in each and every cell of creation. Amma emphasizes that on the path of *Sri Vidya* it is our sacred responsibility to be like the sages of old, who respected and cared for all forms of life—including the very elements themselves--as manifestations of Divinity.

More than a thousand people wanted to attend this *Sri Vidya* retreat with Amma, but less than a hundred people had the privilege of doing so. However, in Her infinite compassion, Amma is making available to everyone, through this book you hold in your hands, the unprecedented blessing of entrance into *Sri Vidya*.

"The gates are open, children," Amma says to us. "Let us all enter this grand mansion of *Sri Vidya*, and be drenched in the flood of its supreme light! Just as everyone is very naturally energized and illumined by the rays of the sun, in the same way, everyone who enters the wondrous mansion of *Sri Vidya* will be flooded and drenched by the light of divine knowledge!"

May all seekers of Truth have the blessing of reading the secrets of *Sri Vidya* revealed by Sri Karunamayi in this beautiful book. May you be inspired by the infinite love and compassion that flows from each word to tread the royal path shown by Her. May all attain the ultimate fulfillment of human life—the experience of Truth and the eternal bliss of Self-Realization! *Jai Karunamayi!*

Manorama Agerwala
Cassia Berman

PRONUNCIATION KEY

All Sanskrit and non-English words (other than proper names and places) are in italics throughout the text. The Shlokas presented in this book have been spelled using the International Standard of Sanskrit Transliteration.

Letter	Sounds Like
a	u in s**u**n
ā	a in f**a**ther
i	i in f**i**ll
ī	ee in f**ee**l
u	u in f**u**ll
ū	oo in f**oo**d
ṛ	ri in **ri**g, *or* roo in b**roo**k
e	ay in m**ay**
ai	ai in **ai**sle
o	o in r**o**se
ow	ow in c**ow**
ung	ung in s**ung**
ḥ	ha in a**ha**
k	k in **k**ite
kh	kh in sil**k h**at
g	g in **g**um
gh	gh in lo**g h**ut
c	ch in **ch**urn
ch	chh in cat**ch h**er
j	j in **j**ug
jh	dgeh in he**dgeh**og
ṭ	t in **t**on
ṭh	th in an**t h**ill

Letter	Sounds Like
ḍ	d in **d**ove
ḍh	dh in Go**dh**ead
t	soft t as in French '*tu*'
th	th in **th**umb
d	th in **the**
dh	theh in brea**the h**ard
n	n in **n**umber
p	p in **p**un
ph	ph in u**ph**ill
b	b in **b**ird
bh	bh as in jo**b h**unt
m	m in **m**other
y	y in **y**earn
r	r in **r**un
l	l in **l**ove
v	v in lo**v**e *or* w in **w**orld
ś	sh in **sh**un - Amma often pronounces this as "sa" or "sya"
ṣ	sh in mar**sh**
s	s in **s**un
h	h in **h**oney
jn	ngy in si**ng y**our

Śrī vidyām jagatām dhātrīm
Sriṣṭi sthiti layeśvarīm
Namāmi lalitām nityām
Mahā tripura sundarīm

"Divine Mother is the cause of creation,
sustenance and dissolution of the universe.
Sri Vidya alone has the answer"— Lord Siva

ॐ

WELCOME TO PENUSILA

Swamiji: *Jai Karunamayi!* I welcome Amma's most beloved children. It is a great divine opportunity for all of you to be in Amma's divine presence today—to be with Amma in Amma's abode. Penusila Ashram is Amma's main ashram. Penusila is in the district of Nellore in Andhra Pradesh. Mother established the ashram here in the year 1980. Before that, during Her childhood, Mother used to visit this place with Her parents and spend a number of days here. In those days there was no transportation as we have now, and in comparison, it was more serene and quiet.

Many pilgrims visit this place on weekends. Nearby is a powerful temple for Goddess Lakshmi and Lord Narasimha, the fourth incarnation of Sri Maha Vishnu. The sacred image there, which is extremely powerful, was not installed by any human being but is self-born. It appeared naturally out of the earth in the form of Lord Narasimha. Whoever comes here spends most of the time in meditation and silence. This place is also the abode of Sri Adi Lakshmi, the consort of Sri Maha Vishnu.

Penusila is in the midst of a dense forest. Some of the trees were cleared to construct the *ashram* and temple you see here now. In this forest at the foot of the hills, there are beautiful valleys, waterfalls and ponds. When we go deep in the forest, we find places where many *rishis* have performed their *tapas,* austerities. That is the reason why this place is said to be especially powerful for *sadhakas,* those on a spiritual journey, who come here with a strong determination to spend their time in spiritual practices like meditation.

This area has been sanctified by the *tapas* of *rishis* and also by the meditation of our beloved Mother for ten years, from 1980 until 1990. At that time there were no structures like we see now; there were only small pathways, and very few people used to live here. Mother used to spend most of Her time in meditation. She would go deep into the forest and become absorbed in meditation. Many of the devotees who came here during that time were inspired and blessed to meditate for a number of days at the Penusila Ashram. They would also go out into the forest and do their meditation.

So the place where you are now has been sanctified and energized by Mother's presence and Mother's *tapas.* And many powerful forms of worship have taken place here, like *yajnas,* sacred fire ceremonies, in which offerings are made to Divine Mother while chanting *Chandi Sapta Shati* or *Sri Lalita Sahasranama,* and *abhishekas,* ritual bathing, of Lord Rudra and Devi.

This very place where you are sitting now was previously an old meditation hall, and in this hall was a very powerful *Sri Chakra*[1] which was worshipped for a number of years. Amma has installed that *Sri Chakra* in the foundation of the place where we're sitting. It has been placed below the ground at the center of this new meditation hall. Mother had predicted that in the future people would come here and have the opportunity to do meditation, that there would be a small meditation hall constructed here. It has happened now after fifteen years!

We are very, very fortunate to be here in Amma's home. Many of you have taken time off from work and

---

[1] *Sri Chakra:* Sacred geometric representation of divine Consciousness. It is a symbol for the energy in the universe and spiritual centers within the human body where this same energy also resides.

traveled thousands of miles to come here, experiencing the physical discomfort of traveling so far. It is not difficult to get to India, but once you reach Bangalore or other cities, getting to Penusila is not easy. This is a remote place, and we are at the end of a long road. The road itself ends just half a kilometer past the *ashram,* at the temple of Lakshmi Devi and Sri Narasimha Swamy. Beyond that are huge mountains. The buses have to turn around and go back; they cannot cross the mountains.

When you come here, you may be tense, under some stress or pressure. But Mother wants all Her children to relax here. She wants to tell all of you that it is not only for meditation that you are here, but you have also come to be in Mother's home.

According to the retreat schedule supplied to you, we request you all to be punctual for all the classes, since there will be a connection in Amma's teachings from one class to another. We have to focus and concentrate our attention on the purpose of our visit here: to spend a few days of our lifetime in a place where many *rishis* have performed *tapas* and where Amma also has done *tapas.* It is a golden time, because this is a very sacred and powerful place.

Mother says that apart from the regular meditation time, if you feel like meditating longer hours, you are most welcome to do that. You can meditate within the premises of the *ashram.* If Mother wishes, and if the weather permits, sometimes we will go into the forest.

Early in the morning after your first round of meditation, which will start at 5:30 a.m. and go on till 6:30 a.m., we will be doing the *surya namaskara,* that is, offering salutations to *Surya Deva,* the Sun God. We will do this at the center of the *ashram* where we have the statue of *Gayatri Devi* in the small *mandapam,* canopy. Everyone is requested to come there and stand in two lines—men in one and women in the other. Water will be supplied to you along with some flower petals. We will be chanting the *Gayatri Mantra* and other *mantras* in front of the Sun God; with each *Gayatri Mantra,* we will offer salutations to *Surya Deva.* There is an elaborate process to do this, but we are doing it in a simpler way, standing in front of the Sun God and offering prayers and *arghya. Arghya* are the oblations that we give to *Surya Deva.* We will take a little water and a few flower petals in our right palm. After reciting the *Gayatri Mantra* once, we will pour the water on the ground. This *surya namaskara* will be repeated three times.

[Swamiji continues to talk about the specifics of the retreat schedule.]

We will be starting our group meditation by chanting *Omkara* nine times. *Omkara* should not come just from the lips but from the bottom of our hearts, starting from the *muladhara chakra,* the root *chakra* located at the base of the spine in the subtle body. Select a comfortable position that you can sit in for a long period of time. The *asana* you choose could be *padmasana, vajrasana, virasana,* etc. Whichever position is most comfortable for you is what is recommended. It is important to stay in the same *asana* throughout one session of meditation. If you get leg pain or cramps and you want to change your position, you may do so without opening your eyes. However, try not to do this more than once or twice, not all the time. If you can sit still for at least an hour without any body movements, that is best, but it requires a little practice.

As Mother has explained in many of Her discourses, during meditation all thoughts are silenced. *"Dhyanam nirvishayam manah:* Freeing the mind from all thoughts is real meditation." During meditation many disconnected thoughts and also unusual thoughts often disturb and distract us. That is quite common for many people. Mother has said that sitting for this noble cause of closing our eyes and going within is not easy—it is the work of Lord Siva!

Dhyana, meditation, was first practiced by Lord Siva. Siva Himself has graced us with this great art of meditation and *tapas*.

So what happens in *tapas?* Being in this world, under the influence of *maya,* we become deeply immersed and entangled in the activities of the world, and sometimes we are misled. We get caught up in *maya,* and this results in *samskaras*[2] or *vasanas.* All these layers of *vasanas* have to be burned, and this is only possible through meditation. This has been clearly stated in the scriptures. When we meditate, all our *samskaras* or *vasanas* are burned.

This is not as easy as it might seem when we discuss it or read about it. When we close our eyes, and when our mind is completely under control, not wandering here and there, at that time in an unseen way all these *vasanas* gradually evaporate. This is not visible to the naked eye. As all these layers of *vasanas* are burned, one becomes established in the inner Self. And that is a different world! One enjoys being in that state or world for a long time, and sometimes one doesn't feel like opening one's eyes. This is the kind of experience we have as we go deeper and deeper in meditation, and slowly our active mind becomes inactive with the regular practice of meditation.

There are different types of meditation; Mother's recommendation is what is called *sahaja,* or the natural way, which is what the *rishis* practiced. But this course is not only about meditation. Amma also graces us with inspiration through Her many teachings from the scriptures,

---

[2] *samskāra, vāsana*: (impression, consequence) Impressions, tendencies or desires, also known as *vasanas,* present in the consciousness that are the result of the individual's thoughts and actions in this life as well as in past births. The sum total of these form a person's character.

and revelations of many secrets that have been discussed by the *rishis*. As we practice meditation, these words of the *Guru* touch the depths of our hearts. Being here in Penusila with Amma is very different from other meditation retreats, because we are not only practicing *sadhana* but we are also listening to divine words of wisdom from Mother.

So when we begin our meditation, we will start by chanting *Omkara* nine times—together, in a melodious voice. After that we will do *pranayama. Pranayama* by itself is a great austerity. Mother recommends *sukha pranayama,* which is simple breath control. *Pranayama* enriches our meditation and increases our power of concentration. *Ekagratha* means concentration, and is very important in meditation. To do any ordinary work in this world we need one-pointed concentration. *Pranayama* enhances our power of concentration.

ॐ

SRI VIDYA IS THE KNOWLEDGE OF MOTHER DIVINE

Swamiji: The subject Mother has chosen for this retreat is *Sri Vidya,* a really unique subject. The very word *"Sri"* means *mangala*—very auspicious. The *Sri bijakshara*, seed letter, is the Lakshmi *bijakshara,* which brings prosperity, divine light, divine wisdom and energy. It has many meanings, and Mother has explained the *Sri bijakshara* to us many times. *Sri Vidya* is the knowledge of Mother Divine. Mother is going to explain *Sri Vidya* to us in many ways. It is a very beautiful subject. This is the first time Mother will be speaking to us about *Sri Vidya,* so we are very fortunate.

To understand *Sri Vidya* is not easy. In ancient times, many *rishis* were well-versed in many other *shastras,* holy scriptures, but could not understand *Sri Vidya*. In order to know *Sri Vidya* one has to approach a *Guru* who has complete knowledge of *Sri Vidya*. Even in ancient times, those *rishis* who knew *Sri Vidya* did not easily impart that knowledge—it was kept secret. Rishi Agastya, a very powerful sage from southern India, was knowledgeable about many things. He wanted to learn about *Sri Vidya* and came to Bhagavan Hayagriva, who was none other than the incarnation of Maha Vishnu. Sri Hayagriva had a human body and the head of a horse. Maharshi Agastya went to Lord Hayagriva's *ashram* and waited there for eighteen long years! He did a lot of *seva* in the *ashram*.

When people come to an *ashram,* not only do they have to learn, but they also have to serve there.This place where Agastya Maharshi went and waited for Hayagriva Bhagavan, and also did his penance, is called Mercara, and is very close to Bangalore. It is a very beautiful place at the top of the mountains. To get there, one has to cross the mountains and pass through the source of the Kaveri River in the district of Coorg. From there the river flows through the hills, through the state of Karnataka into Tamil Nadu, and then finally reaches the ocean.

This year Mother wanted to take all of you there, but since it has been raining heavily, it would not have been easy to reach. We would have to go through the mountain ranges, and it is always wet there. There are cardamom plantations, and other spices grow in the area. It is also very cold; the temperatures are around ten to twenty degrees Celsius. The clouds touch the mountains and it is very scenic. Maybe we will take that trip another year.

Mercara is the place where Agastya Maharshi was blessed with the knowledge of *Sri Vidya* and *Sri Lalita Sahasranama*. He waited there so patiently. So what does this tell us of Agastya Maharshi? Even though he was a *maharshi,* he waited for so many long years, doing *seva*—washing clothes, cleaning huge cooking pots, picking vegetables and fruits, and laboring in many other ways. Why did the *Gurus* wait so long before giving their teachings? Because they first tested the patience, dedication and self-control of the disciples. Only then would they impart their knowledge.

So the knowledge of *Sri Vidya* is very rare to obtain. Only a few *rishis* acquired it. This is because there were few suitable disciples to receive this wonderful knowledge. As *Sri Vidya* is very powerful and secret, the disciples had to be elevated souls with an intense thirst to receive this divine knowledge. So we are very blessed indeed to listen to Mother as She teaches us the importance and significance of *Sri Vidya*. This is a very rare opportunity we are all being given.

ॐ

SRI VIDYA IS THE HIGHEST KNOWLEDGE

Śrī vidyām jagatām dhātrīm sriṣṭi sthiti layeśvarīm
Namāmi lalitām nityām mahā tripura sundarīm

Yā devī sarva bhūteṣu śakti rūpeṇa samsthitā
Namastasyai namastasyai namastasyai namo namaḥ

Embodiments of Divine Souls, Amma's Most Beloved Children,

I love you millions and millions of times, billions and billions of times, trillions and trillions of times! I am very glad to see you all here in Penusila. I know how tired you are after the long journey, so relax here, children. This is your Mom's home. Be free here. Put all your problems aside and just contemplate on the divine Consciousness.

Today we will start *Sri Vidya*. *Sri Vidya* was mentioned in the ancient times by the holy *rishis:*

Śrī vidyām jagatām dhātrīm

"O Mother! You are the *vidya,* the knowledge, of *Atma Vidya,* knowledge of the Soul, *Maha Vidya,* the highest knowledge, *Sri Vidya,* the luminous knowledge of divine Consciousness, and *Moksha Vidya,* the knowledge that leads to liberation."

Moksha Vidya is the knowledge of the Eternal—the true education by which we realize our supreme Self. The education we get in the world, with degrees from colleges and universities, is different. That education is just good for earning money to live comfortably in the world. But this education is called *Moksha Vidya* and gives us liberation. It gives us the highest salvation, which is liberation from the body, mind and the world. With the knowledge of *Sri Vidya,* we are completely liberated from all these bondages and we become totally at peace.

This *vidya* is praised by the holy *rishis* as *Atma Vidya*, the knowledge of the supreme Soul. It gives us the highest knowledge—not knowledge about materialistic things, but about the cosmos, about this universe, about the supreme Self and all divinity. It is a priceless treasure.

"*Sri*" means "treasure." What is this treasure? The treasure is hidden inside. That is why *Sri Vidya* opens with the *Khadga Mala*. All the secrets of the universe are hidden in the *Khadga Mala*. Whenever we chant those *bija mantras* we are connected with the highest knowledge of the supreme Self. So here *Sri Vidya* means *Moksha Vidya, Atma Vidya, Maha Vidya. Maha* signifies the highest education in the world. Knowledge about the supreme Soul is *Atma Vidya* and *Moksha Vidya*. *Moksha* means liberation, salvation—liberation from all the bondages of mind, body, intellect and worldly things. We are completely purified and are totally in our supreme Self. That is *Sri*.

So *Sri* is a divine treasure, not material treasure but eternal, everlasting treasure. It is the greatest treasure in the entire world—much more precious than money, gold, diamonds or gems, which belong to the external world. This treasure gives us divine attributes, so that we are able to think of God and of our Self. When we think of our Self whenever we do meditation, all our lower natures subside. Even though we are entangled in *maya* and caught up in the sense of "I," "me" and "mine," through the practice of meditation, all these lower natures fall away and the higher attributes bloom in our inner garden. So this education is the eternal education—everlasting and pure knowledge which gives boundless happiness and bliss. That is *Sri Vidya*.

My dear children, relax. Relax from all the problems in life. This is the modern age and we are immersed in selfishness. Every day we find there is some good and some bad everywhere—in our hearts, in our homes, in the world. So try to see only the pearls and not the shells. Forget about the shells and only see the pearls inside the shell. We are connected with the supreme Oneness. It is already inside, within us, but we don't feel the connection because of the three cages—the mind, body and intellect. Whenever we forget these three and are connected with the inner Self, we experience the highest *ananda*, bliss, in meditation.

Vedanta speaks of the good and bad *karma* from previous births. When the previous *karmas* return as merits, it is called *punya;* otherwise, if it is not good, we call it bad *karma*. It is like software. We have innumerable programs installed within us. When we open the program, if the *karma* load is good, our goal will be to discover the secret of life.

In the opening of the *Rig Veda*, the holy *rishis* have suggested that one can continue to search for Reality in the outer world and in the inner world. This search is called *anveshana*. It is a very sweet Sanskrit word. Since the beginning of the world, all the holy people have been searching for the secret: "What is the purpose of my life? Where is *ananda*, bliss? What can I do in this world? How is my life connected with all the external things in this world?" With such questions in their minds, they have been searching for the secret of happiness and peace in the external world as well as in the inner world.

There are two worlds. One is the external world, which is beautiful and is the creation of Divine Mother. It is not the creation of man, but men with their own hands have spoiled this world with all kinds of pollutants, such as mind and thought pollution, chemical pollution, global radiation, etc. The other world is the inner world. Because of our previous good deeds, the inner world is purified and in this inner, pure world we are searching for the secret of "I-ness." "Who am I? What is the purpose of my life?" So we are searching and searching and constantly searching. Finally we are able to experience the highest bliss in our life. That is *Sri Vidya*, the eternal education.

It is mentioned in the scriptures that the first disciples of *Sri Vidya* were Lord Siva, Sri Maha Vishnu, Brahma, Kubera,[3] and the Sun God. They all started meditating on the supreme Self through *Sri Vidya* only. Later, Lopamudra Devi, her husband Agastya Muni, and Durvasa Rishi also practiced *Sri Vidya,* meditated and attained Self-Realization. Other holy *rishis* obtained the knowledge of *Sri Vidya* from them.

Yesterday we visited the Sri Kalahasti Temple, and I asked the people there about the cost of one temple pillar. They said, "Amma, carved pillars like these are not available in India anymore. Just look at the stone! It would cost millions, and there are a thousand such pillars in this temple." It is difficult to build a temple now. These days we do not have such finely detailed sculpture—only the faces of the deities in the temples are carved. The images are covered up with *saris* and ornaments so that only their faces are visible. Nowadays we do not have sculptures like those seen in the temples in Belur and Halebidu. However, we still have the need for treasures, you know.

Now only one treasure remains in our life, and that treasure is the eternal treasure—*Atma Vidya*, *Maha Vidya*. Everyone has the right to meditate on the supreme Self. So we need to travel on the path of Truth to experience supreme Consciousness and fulfill our destiny. Amma's desire is that her children travel on the path of Truth and attain Realization. Realize your Self. Be in your Self. Be

---

[3] Kubera: Treasurer of the Gods.

always in your Self. Remain in the world but be in supreme Consciousness, in the consciousness of *Sri Vidya*, which is eternal Consciousness. Do not be in material consciousness or bodily consciousness or worldly consciousness. We need the consciousness of the holy *rishis,* who in the four stages[4] are always in one consciousness. They are very quiet, very silent inside. They have no thoughts. They are in absolute silence. They experience the highest bliss inside and are totally in that Consciousness only. That is *Sri Vidya*.

Children, this is a very sacred place. Here the holy Garudachala Mountains are connected with the Tirumala and the Sri Sailam Mountains. In India we find that people have a lot of material poverty. So what can they do? The treasures of the people are the temples and scriptures only. People are deceived by their mind, their intellect and by others; they are deceived by their aggressive nature, and by this world. They don't care for life. This is due to the *karma* load from their previous lives. Wherever we may be, let us pray to Mother Divine for inner peace and eternal happiness. We need to pray to Mother Divine for eternal happiness, at least. You may have witnessed, if you have been to the remote villages of India and seen people's lifestyles, problems, trials and tribulations, that there is nothing in their external lives. It is empty. But when I speak to thousands of such people during the interviews and healing time, I find that they are very contented inside. The spiritual treasure of these people is inner peace. Everyone

---

[4] The four stages: The states of consciousness or awareness. They are classified as: 1. *jāgrat,* waking; 2. *svapnā,* dreaming; 3. *sushupti,* deep sleep; 4. *turiyā,* beyond these three—the thought-free state of *samādhi.* A fifth stage, *turyātita* (i.e., beyond even *turiyā*), is when a *yogi* stays continuously in the bliss of supreme Consciousness, totally unaware of the body or the manifested universe, having merged with and become the Absolute.

needs this peace. We need to share our peace with the whole world.

So, my dear babies, wake up from your sleep! That "I-ness," "me-ness" and "my-ness" is part of this dream which we have been dreaming for innumerable births. Now we want to realize our supreme Self. When your supreme Self comes out of this body made of *pancha bhutas*, the five elements, the little mind, and the little intellect, it touches the cosmos! You are all-pervasive. You belong to everyone. Everybody belongs to your Self. You never differentiate: "This is my country, that is your country." Some people in the U.S. come and ask me, "Amma, are you free, are you comfortable in our country?" "Son, this is also my country." I really love everybody and feel that everyone belongs to me. This is my strong feeling and experience. I never see any differences between your country and my country, because in the spiritual world one is beyond these barriers. Everyone in the entire universe belongs to your supreme Self.

What is *Sri Vidya?* When *Sri*, the real supreme Self, comes out of the three cages, your subtle body expands and touches the cosmos; you are all-pervasive, you yourself are that oneness, you yourself are absolute bliss, you yourself are the highest *ananda,* and you yourself are the supreme *Omkara*. All these millions, billions and trillions of universes are in you only, in your supreme Self. Gods, Goddesses, human beings, flowers, trees, insects, plants and all existence is in your heart. You are the supreme Being! So we need that kind of meditation, and this is the perfect place to do it.

Yesterday we had the *darshan* of the seven holy *rishis* during our visit to the Kalahasti Temple. But we didn't have much time to cover everything, and people were talking too much; it was not silent in the temple. Where are the holy *rishis*? The seven holy *rishis* physically exist there in the Kalahasti Temple. They brought and installed the seven holy *lingas.*[5] Sri Rama also installed a huge *linga* there. So did Sita and Lakshmana. And even *Sri Anjaneya,* Lord Hanuman, installed a small *linga* to show his deep devotion for Sri Rama. It is not a big *linga;* it is a small one. The Fire God came in human form and installed a *linga* there, too. There are innumerable *lingas* in the temple. There are innumerable things to see in the temple of *Jnana prasunambika*. In the northeast corner there is a small *Sri Yantra* [6] which is the life of the temple. Actually we wanted to go and meditate there, but there were so many people in *darshan* lines and people were talking, so there was a lot of disturbance. There are many things to see in that temple.

What is a temple? It is faith. Throughout the town, people are suffering with poverty, but the temple is very rich. There are so many encroachments around the temple. People depend on the temple, their living depends on the temple, the entire town depends on the temple. That is what a temple is. It is nothing but faith only.

The Kalahasti Temple is called *Jalandhara pitha*. There, Divine Mother resides as *Jalandhara pitha nivasini Jnana prasunamba*. Mother, *Amba,* is *jnana*, divine knowledge, eternal knowledge. And this Mother is called *Prasuna*, which means the thousand petal lotus. This thousand petal lotus is *jnana*—the fragrant flower of

---

[5] *linga:* A highly venerated symbol of the inexpressible nature of the divine Lord Siva, that in which the universe moves and into which it is absorbed. Its elliptical shape is reminiscent of the orbits of the planets, i.e., all movement in the cosmos, and also of a flame of light, the light of Consciousness. There are twelve sacred *linga pithas* (holy centers) in India.

[6] *Sri Yantra:* A two-dimensional geometric diagram of the sacred *Sri Chakra*.

supreme knowledge. The place where the temple now stands was a holy place before the time of the *Rig Veda*. It was there that the celestial King Indra meditated and experienced Mother Divine; this incident is told in the *Kenopanishad*. In a conversation between *Guru* and *shishya*, disciple, in which the *Guru* was Mother Divine—who was not in the physical form but in the form of light—Mother spoke in his heart. He never saw Her physically, but all the responses came to him in his heart, and he experienced eternal light within. He meditated for many years. He even gave up his position as king. He just wanted to know the Truth. This incident happened there.

The *Siva linga* at the Kalahasti Temple is so beautiful. There is also a story that the Divine gave salvation there to a spider. We think that in all creation, salvation is only for humankind. But in God's eye, salvation is also for a spider, an elephant, a snake, as well as for a simple, illiterate tribal man. They don't know any *mantras,* they do not have knowledge of the scriptures; all they have is love towards the Divine. That is enough.

You can be inspired by this. Have a little bit of love. We are not *rishis*, we are ordinary human beings. We are always on the run in the 21st century, the computer age. We experience so much confusion, commotion, trials and tribulations. We suffer from health problems, so we cannot sit in meditation for ages like holy *rishis*. But we have love, and we also want to do meditation. We have come all the way here for that purpose.

My dear, most beloved babies, we have this rare opportunity. This is a divine call to you. It is not an ordinary call—it is a very special call. You came all the way here with pain in your heart. You have a lot of problems in your life, but you have set them all aside and come here to this holy place and are meditating on Mother Divine in your heart. You want the experience of eternal joy. So I bless you, my babies. I expect the highest *ananda*, bliss, for you. You are my children and you can meditate well. Contemplate more and more on Divinity. Be one with your supreme Self. Everything is inside.

The inner world, *dahar akasha,* is a place of eternal happiness, peace and joy. We have two worlds—this external world, which you can leave to one side, and the inner world, which is the world of eternal happiness, eternal joy and inner silence. Everything is in this inner world only. In Sanskrit we call it by a beautiful name, *dahar akasha. Akasha* means sky. When Mother appears in the *dahar akasha*, we call Her *Dahar akasha rupini.* Trillions and gazillions of suns, stars and fires put together are also not equal to that light. That is your Self. You are not this body, you are not this mind, and you are not born. This is just a drama. We are in this play. Why are we entangled in this play? We need to realize that this is only a play, then we will be connected with the supreme eternal bliss and happiness.

A thousand years ago, the temples in Belur and Halebidu belonged to the whole world. The sculptures in those temples are really beyond beautiful, they are indescribable. The sculptors who worked on them dedicated their entire lives to sculpture, never expecting any comforts for themselves. Imagine their dedication! We need that kind of dedication to spirituality.

So my dear, most beloved children, mentally dedicate your entire life to that divine purpose, which is Truth. Where is this Truth? This Truth is within us. This Truth is nothing but *Sri Vidya* only. This *vidya,* knowledge, is very sacred and very secret. Very secret! During the time of the *Rig Veda*, only about ten people, not all the people, knew about *Sri Vidya.* They were Brahma the creator, Rudra, who was the first meditator, Maha Vishnu, Indra, Durvasa, and the holy *rishis,* who meditated for so many years on the

Truth and realized that *Sri Vidya* alone was true knowledge. To meditate upon the supreme Self is the real *vidya*. *Vidya* means education—the eternal education. All the holy *rishis* dedicated their entire lives to this eternal education. They finally realized it and revealed this path to deserving seekers. And that is what true education is—to realize the supreme Self.

In the *vedic* times there were many rivers. Now many rivers have disappeared. Between Bangalore and here, twenty years ago we had at least ten to fifteen rivers. In the past few years, even those have disappeared. When we first came here, we had the beautiful Kanvamukhi River. All the rivers are disappearing and so is the greenery. Purity is disappearing from the world. Yesterday many people were asking, "Amma, is there any hope in this world? Can we ever have eternal peace in our world?" Every time I say, "My dear children, I have hope. We need to work together in this world to control this mental and physical pollution with our spirituality, with our meditation."

If you are a really good meditator, you are more than a sun, more than a million suns. With your inner light, you can bring peace to the United States, Africa, Japan and every country. We can bring peace and control the negative powers in society. We can bring people together, help them unite with love and control their negativity.

I have hope for all this and I am working for that purpose. I also expect that from my children in this meditation course. Meditation opens your heart. We are not closed-hearted. We are more open in our real understanding, in our knowledge about society and its problems, pains and negativities. If you have real love and openness inside, you are in tune with the entire world and you are one with the eternal cosmic Consciousness. *Sri Vidya* is a beautiful subject. We are going to discuss all these things in our course, my dear children.

You can relax in Amma's home. If you want to eat something you can give us your menu and there are people who will attend to your comfort. You can ask us. Mom's home is everyone's home. So first, relax from all of your pains and any problems—money problems, health problems or any other problem. Just forget about them for at least this week, in this meditation retreat. Just relax and be like a small baby. Pray, meditate, and enjoy the meditation.

The holy *rishis* knew the truth about this ever-changing world. This world is not constant and it is not permanent. It is always on the wheels of change. Our mind is continuously changing. Everything that is changing is impermanent. Eternal *Omkara* is the only absolute Truth. Only that is changeless. That is the supreme Consciousness—without attributes, beyond this world, beyond the three *gunas* or natures—*sattva, rajas* and *tamas*—beyond our mind, body and intellect, beyond everything in this ever-changing world. That Consciousness is permanent, all-pervasive. So we need the experience of that supreme *ananda* and Truth in our meditation.

So my dear children, in your daily life you do not get the opportunity to close your eyes and meditate for a long duration. The phone calls, like tyrants, are always behind your back. You need to do this and that. The pressure of work is there. Here, you have no pressure. Here you are in the lap of Mother Nature. Around us we have four hundred acres of forest land. This is a forest. The Government of India has given us permission to build the *ashram* and temple here, but generally people are not allowed to construct anything here.

So children, you came all the way here for the purpose of meditation. You can contemplate on the supreme Self and give all your problems and pain to Amma. Put them in Amma's lap. Amma will burn all the problems. I want to see you children relaxed and spiritually enlightened in this birth itself. This is a very special opportunity, like that of the celestial King Indra, who gave up his kingdom and came all the way to Kalahasti and meditated there for innumerable years to attain salvation. Finally he got liberation through the grace of Mother Divine.

This is Mother's place. It is actually Lord Narasimha's place, but before Narasimha, it belonged to Maha Lakshmi, the Goddess of the wealth of spirituality. We have every kind of wealth and we are content. We are not asking Mother for more money, but we pray, "O Mother, we are imploring You like beggars for salvation, liberation from our aggressive natures, liberation from our inner enemies, liberation from worldly attachments, liberation from all the lower natures. Mother, give me liberation instantly, I implore you and I beg you. Mother, remove all these black curtains from my heart and open my heart. I want to experience the light inside in the *dahar akasha*—the inner Self."

Viśvasya bījam paramāsi māyā

This is a beautiful prayer *shloka*. Who is Mother Divine? *Vishvasya bijam*. There is a seed for this entire universe. Mother is that seed. From that seed all the universes are born. From the source of that supreme Consciousness,

Viśvasya bījam paramāsi māyā

"Without Your energy it is impossible to sustain this entire cosmos. You alone sustain this whole cosmos with Your energy, with Your light, with Your Self. Therefore I cannot say that You are mother, father, or this or that. You are *sakara,* manifest, in all these innumerable forms. All these forms are Mother only—female forms, male forms, tree forms, grass, stones, pebbles, rivers, oceans, all forms.

But I do not have the eye to see that light. O Mother, open my third eye! I want to see You everywhere, I want to experience the all-pervasiveness of Mother Consciousness in each and every atom of this entire cosmos. Mother, open my heart!" This is the prayer in this *shloka:*

Śrī vidyām jagatām dhātrīm sriṣṭi sthiti layeśvarīm
Namāmi lalitām nityām mahā tripura sundarīm

Śrī vidyām jagatām dhātrīm: Entire universes come from this light only, the very source of all energy. That is *Sri Vidya*. *Sri Vidya* is nothing but *Omkara*.

Sriṣṭi sthiti layeśvarīm: You are the cause of this entire universe. You sustain this entire universe. The entire universe merges back into You.

Namāmi lalitām nityām: Mother, you are eternal. I'm calling you "Mother," but You are not mother, You are not father—You are eternal. You are light, the light that illumines the universe. You are the source of the entire universe, of the whole cosmos. You are my supreme Self.

We come across beautiful names of Mother Divine, such as *Lalita Parameshwari* and *Lalita Tripura sundari*. What is the meaning of *Lalita? Lalita* consists of three syllables: *la*, *li* and *ta*. *La* represents *layam,* dissolution. It is the *bijakshara* which dissolves or merges. Actually, the individual ultimately has to merge with the Supreme or the Divine. When we merge, we must merge completely, like a river that merges with the ocean and then loses its separate identity as a river. *Li* denotes that which is beyond the genders of masculine or feminine. *Ta* is the *Taraka Mantra,* the redeeming *mantra, Omkara.* So *Lalita,* this beautiful name of the supreme Mother or Divine Mother, is the very name into which we get completely absorbed. Having absorbed everything, going beyond gender differences of male and female, Mother confers *moksha*. Therefore, She is referred to as *Lalita Tripura sundari,* which means that She is the embodiment of all the three Goddesses—Lakshmi Devi, Saraswati Devi and Parvati Devi—meditating upon whom, one attains liberation. She is *Para Brahma chaitanya,* the eternal consciousness of the Absolute.

This is the meaning of this *dhyana shloka* for *Maha Tripura sundari. Sri Vidya* is like the password for this *shloka. Sri Vidya* is the eternal *vidya*—the *vidya* for salvation. This supreme education purifies our inner self, gives us wisdom, and the experience of eternity.

ॐ

SRI VIDYA LEADS TO MOKSHA

Śrī vidyām jagatām dhātrīm sṛṣṭi sthiti layeśvarīm
Namāmi lalitām nityām mahā tripura sundarīm

Om śānti śanti śantiḥ

Lokāḥ samastāḥ sukhino bhavantu

Om Hrīmkārāsana garbhitānala śikhām
Sauḥ klīm kalām bibhratīm
Sauvarṇāmbara dhāriṇīm vara sudhām
Dhautām trinetrojjvalām
Vande pustaka pāśamānkuśa dharām
Srag bhūṣitām ujjvalām
Tvām gaurīm tripurām parātpara kalām
Śrī cakra sancāriṇīm

Embodiments of Divine Souls, Amma's Most Beloved Children,

The word *"Sri"* means "grand and indivisible divine splendor." It also indicates prosperity. *"Vidya"* is "education or knowledge." *Sri Vidya* is the highest learning, which leads to *moksha,* liberation. That is why Amma has chosen the wonderful subject of *Sri Vidya* for this meditation retreat.

Srim is the most important *bijakshara,* seed letter, in *Sri Vidya.* It is the glowing crown of *Sri Vidya. Srim bijakshara* is *jnana*, supreme knowledge, *Srim* is *moksha,* liberation, *Srim* is indivisible radiance.

The great scripture *Lalita Sahasranama* speaks about *Sri Vidya* in several of the thousand names of Divine

Mother. *Sri Vidya* is also called *Maha Vidya,* the highest knowledge, *Atma Vidya,* knowledge of the Self, *Brahma Vidya,* knowledge of supreme Consciousness, the Absolute, and *Moksha Vidya,* knowledge that leads to the eternal bliss of liberation.

Here is a question: "Why do we need to know about the Self?" Ordinary people often think that spiritual seekers are simply wasting their lives in meditation and other spiritual practices. [Laughter] They cannot see the necessity of *Atma Vidya,* Self–knowledge, knowledge of the Truth.

Amma will answer the question. *Sri Vidya* is not new. It has been handed down to us through time immemorial by Brahma, Vishnu and *Maheshwara*, the deities of the Trinity who have the power to create, preserve and dissolve creation. They turned inward in meditation and came to know this *Vidya*. And what is this *Sri Vidya?* It is the knowledge and awareness that there is a light within everyone. This light is not an ordinary light, as we all know. The light within us is nothing but the Self, or *Atma.* It has the power to drench the entire cosmos with its radiance. It gives light to the entire creation. That is the power hidden within each and every soul.

The knowledge of the power, energy or light hidden within all living beings is called *Brahma Vidya, Atma Vidya* or *Sri Vidya*. This is the *Vidya* which the *Vedas* give, and which the *rishis* also realized. They hold it out to us so that we, too, can experience this supreme light if we meditate. Those who are fortunate enough and blessed enough to come onto the path of spirituality and do *sadhana* finally realize their own Self as the light within them. It is the search for that light that draws seekers all over the world to spirituality.

The *Vedas* have no origin. From the beginning of humanity's time on Earth, the *Vedas* have taught us how to live a happy and peaceful life. These scriptures do not have any authorship—one cannot say that the *Vedas* were written by any one person. The truths in the *Vedas* were revealed to pure souls who had performed intense *sadhana* and attained knowledge of the Self. These sages taught what they had learned to deserving disciples, and in this way the sacred teachings passed from one generation to the next.

The light within everyone is incomparable and unexplainable. Yet we are always entangled in the endless problems and difficulties of life. The *Vedas* say that life should not be like this—it should be peaceful and calm. We can have peace if we know about the light within. *Sri Vidya* gives us *Atma Vidya,* knowledge of the divine inner light—the light that envelops all creation, illuminating billions of galaxies in the cosmos! This is *Maha Vidya,* the greatest knowledge.

Sri Vidya has always been very secret. It was imparted only to a few very dedicated seekers. However, this sacred knowledge of the *Atman* should be available to all, and everyone should have the opportunity to experience the light of the Self. That is why Amma wishes to teach everyone about this *Maha Vidya*. The *Vedas* do not belong to any particular culture, religion, caste, color, creed or region; they belong to the entire world, and are beyond the universe, too. They belong to everyone. Every human being has the right to attain knowledge of the Truth.

How can one achieve Self-knowledge? There is only one way to attain this ultimate goal of *Atma Vidya* and the experience of divine inner light, and that is the royal road of *dhyana*—meditation. To progress in meditation, it is important to have a *Guru* who can guide us to follow the path of *dharma,* and bring us to a high level of spiritual awareness. This guidance is important, because life is not smooth. We all know how many disturbances we have in our lives—not just every day, but every moment. Our lives are filled with *ashanti,* commotion, not peace.

Like a loving mother, the *Vedas* bless all beings with these *mantras,* showing us how they would like our lives to be:

Sarveti sukhinaḥ santu
May everyone in all of creation be happy.

Svastibhir prajābhiḥ
May the benediction of auspiciousness be showered on all beings in creation.

Lokāḥ samastāḥ sukhino bhavantu
May everyone in all realms be happy.

The *Vedas* are nothing but light—its brilliance and effulgence. Their vision is universal. They are unique–they bless everyone in creation. They wish peace for all beings. It is Amma's wish that at least for one fraction of a second, everyone should be aware that the *Vedas* have been blessing us right from the beginning. It is Amma's most heartfelt wish that you come out of this *maya,* see the light that is within you, and shed all these shackles of *avidya,* this darkness in which you have become entangled. Know that the *Vedas* are watching over you, guiding you, leading you to the path of Truth.

We are in this world, on Mother Earth. She is supporting us, giving us vegetation and water and everything we need for our lives. But how many of us think of Mother Earth with love? Some say that there is life only on Mother Earth. But with all she gives us, do we think about Mother Earth at all? Do we say prayers of gratitude?

The same is true of the Sun God, who gives us so much energy in the form of light and heat. Just imagine the world without the sun! It's dark now, but we know that in several hours the sun's rays will be here again. Without light, there would be no life on Earth. Sunlight destroys bacteria, not only from the environment, but also from our hair, skin and clothing, and helps keep us healthy. The sun is giving us so much, but we don't think about the sun or show our gratitude.

Just as Mother Earth and the sun do so much for us who are living here on this Earth, so the *Vedas*, right from the beginning—from time immemorial, even before this creation—have been anticipating our lives and praying for us, for the welfare and prosperity of all.

Sarve sukhinah santu: Let all creatures have peace and contentment—not just a few people, or people who belong to one family or one country, but the whole creation.

Lokah samasta sukhino bhavantu: Lokah doesn't mean just one particular region. It means the entire creation must be happy, prosperous and in peace.

So every human being needs to be aware, if only for a second, how much the *Vedas* have been thinking about us.

Sri Vidya teaches us that everyone should meditate during *suprabhata. "Su"* means "very good, auspicious," and *"prabhata"* means "dawn." The best time for meditation is before sunrise. The *Brahmi muhurta* is from 3:30 to 4:30 a.m. *Suprabhata* continues from 4:30 to 6:00 a.m. Even scientists are coming to know about the importance of this early morning time. Recently a devotee gave me a newspaper article about a scientist who said that morning enhances the brain, making it active and energetic.

Sometimes people suffer from depression, which can last for a number of years. Many young people commit suicide; it is so sad. Don't get into depression. Early morning meditation chases away depression. If you cannot meditate, at least let the light of the rising sun fall on your body for a minimum of ten minutes. A morning walk will also energize the brain and nervous system.

The *Vedas* speak of the *pancha bhutas,* the five elements in nature—ether, air, fire, water and earth. The ancient *rishis* could see how their vital energy flowed through all creation. That is why they worshipped the elements. The wonderful teaching of the *Vedas* says that we need these elements in our lives, so we must safeguard them. Instead, with our own hands, we have ruined our life here on Earth by polluting the elements. But the worst pollution of all is thought pollution. Perhaps we no longer worship the five elements, but our early morning meditation, performed regularly, can help safeguard the *pancha bhutas* and control the pollution around us. This is what *Sri Vidya* tells us.

Meditation is very powerful. It helps the individual as well as society. A serious meditator once visited a mental hospital where the patients couldn't control their behavior. These patients became silent when the meditator was with them. Anyone who meditates has that spiritual power. Meditators carry a special form of energy with them. This energy goes with them wherever they are and has a calming effect on others. That is why, when we sit in front of *mahatmas,* holy people, we feel so much peace. This is known as *sannidhi shanti. "Sannidhi"* means "being close to, being near," and *"shanti"* is "peace." Sometimes they don't speak with us, but just being in their presence, the mind becomes silent and we feel peaceful.

Daily meditation purifies us and gives us good health. The positive energy we generate in meditation affects the thoughts of others. It helps our family as well as society.

This morning, we spoke about *nirantara anveshana. "Nirantara"* means "always and forever," and *"anveshana,"* "search or inquiry." We have always been seeking true happiness. It is a never-ending journey. We have searched everywhere for many lives and traveled endless miles. Now, due to the good deeds performed in past births, we have been blessed with the opportunity to listen to the teachings of *Sri Vidya*. We have come to know that the light we have been seeking is within us! *Sri Vidya* gives us the experience of that divine light. To describe that light as very powerful is inadequate. It is indestructible and indivisible. *Sri Vidya* teaches us how to become one with the light. It leads us away from the darkness of ignorance into the light of knowledge, and brings us everlasting joy.

Today, we have everything—cars, electricity, so many modern conveniences—but we're still not happy. In *vedic* times, in the era of the *Rig Veda,* life was very simple and quiet. The *rishis* were searching for the secret behind creation. They realized in their meditations that behind the sun, moon, Mother Earth, and all the five elements, there is an eternal energy, an infinite light. If Mother Earth is not happy with us, we can't be happy.

In the time of the *Rig Veda*, when people needed wood to perform a *yajna* or *homa,* before cutting a tree, they prayed to Mother Nature for forgiveness. They planted a thousand cuttings from its branches to grow a thousand new trees. Mother Nature was more dear to them than anyone else in the world.

At that time, people could communicate with all forms of life. The rivers were as revered as their own biological mothers. There is a beautiful story about Visvamitra Muni. When he was a king, before he attained Self-Realization, he once wanted to cross a river with his army. He spoke to the river humbly, "O Mother River, I don't want to touch you with my feet." The river receded, so that he and his army could walk across without soiling the waters, which King Visvamitra held sacred. Such was the intimate communication between Mother Nature and human beings. Today there is no such closeness.

Divinity is everywhere. Now, in this *Kali Yuga,* we never find it, not even within ourselves. It's not general knowledge, like math and science. Today we are constantly running, running, chasing material pleasures. We need to come out of this net of *maya* with our meditation. In the early morning, the atmosphere is charged with cosmic energy. At sunrise we offer salutations to *Surya,* the Sun God, with the *Gayatri Mantra*. When we chant this sacred *mantra*, we pray:

Dhiyo yonaḥ pracodayāt: May my mind and intellect always be filled with divine light and focused on supreme Consciousness.

Doing *Surya namaskara* with the *Gayatri Mantra* connects us to the energy of supreme cosmic Consciousness. All knowledge and inspiration come from the supreme Self.

The *Vedas* do not only worship nature and the elements, they also praise man, for they know that his soul is divine. The *Vedas* say, "Ordinary people are extraordinary to me." Mother *Veda* worships the common person as divine. Amma also sees you all as divine souls. That is why I travel in the world.

Many people criticize the *Vedas,* saying they are full of boring stories. These people do not understand the message behind the words of the *Vedas*. They bless us not for material happiness but for eternal bliss, which can only be achieved through meditation. This boundless treasure is hidden in each and every cell of this body.

Take Amma's words seriously and meditate daily. In the early morning, when most people are sleeping, the atmosphere is not so full of negative thoughts. At that time, when the environment is charged with positive cosmic energy, *pranayama* touches the *kundalini* in the *muladhara chakra* and all the *chakras* get stimulated. Take your *sadhana* seriously, children, and meditate with intensity and love. Meditate for *jnana,* not for the fulfillment of desires.

There are stages in spirituality. In the first stage of spirituality, we do not have much intensity in our *sadhana;*

in the second, there is more intensity. Amma expects more and more intensity in your meditation. Meditate seriously and become absorbed in your Self. Be detached in your separate world with intense meditation. Be like a fragrant water lily, untouched by the smelly mud pond of this world!

If Divine Mother does not allow us, we can never meditate. But with Her grace, we can go into deep meditation even in the middle of a crowd. Mother *Sri Vidya* inspires us to meditate.

Amma wants to see you all in that eternal bliss. You cannot experience it with casual meditation, but only when you are one hundred percent absorbed in *dhyana*. Take care of your health, eat and rest well, and meditate without any thoughts in this beautiful forested area. Tomorrow we will go deeper into the subject of *Sri Vidya.*

ॐ

SRI VIDYA: PRACTICES AND QUALIFICATIONS

Swamiji: *Jai Karunamayi!* We will repeat the beautiful *shlokas* which Mother has dictated to us. We will be starting our classes with these *shlokas*.

At this time Amma is going to tie the holy sacred thread to our right wrist. One by one you will come, and then as you step forward, raise your right hand so that Mother can tie the sacred *diksha* thread.

[Group chanting of *shlokas* while Amma ties the *diksha* thread. This is followed by chanting of *Samputita Sri Suktam*[7]]

Śrī vidyām jagatām dhātrīm sriṣṭi sthiti layeśvarīm
Namāmi lalitām nityām mahā tripura sundarīm....3x

Om śānti śanti śantiḥ

Amma: Embodiments of Divine Soul, Amma's Most Beloved Children,

Sri Vidya consists of three different practices. The first one is the *Pancha Dashakshari Mantra japa*. This *mantra* is very powerful. When *Sri Vidya upasakas,* those who worship Divine Mother according to *Sri Vidya,* are initiated into this *mantra,* they make a commitment to practice the *Pancha Dashakshari Mantra* every day for the rest of their lives. The second practice is the daily chanting of *Sri Lalita Sahasranama,* the thousand names of Mother Divine. And the third is the *Sri Chakra archana*—worship of the *Sri*

---

[7] *Samputitā Śrī Sūktam* chanting book and CD available at www.karunamayi.org.

Chakra every day. All three together make up *Sri Vidya upasana.*

How is one to practice *Sri Vidya?* Early in the morning, at 3 a.m., those who practice *Sri Vidya* do *Pancha Dashakshari Mantra japa*, *mantra* meditation. During sunrise, they do *Lalita Sahasranama parayana,* or recitation. And immediately after that, they worship the *Sri Chakra.* All these three together—*mantra japa* at 3 a.m., *Lalita Sahasranama parayana* at approximately 6 in the morning, and immediately after that, *Sri Chakra archana*—make up *Sri Vidya upasana,* the practice of *Sri Vidya.*

This may lead one to think that *Sri Vidya* consists of performing external *puja* and worship. But *Sri Lalita Sahasranama,* which praises Divine Mother as *Sri Vidya* and *Maha Vidya,* also praises Divine Mother as *Antara mukha samaradhya, bahir mukha sudurlabha.*[8] *Antara mukha* is the inwardness we need to truly approach Divine Mother. But whatever external and internal practice we do, it is all *sadhana,* spiritual practice, of *Sri Vidya.*

Sri Vidya is also known as *Shuddha Vidya. Shuddha* is that which purifies. For example, when we use *agni,* fire, ceremonially, it purifies everything. In the same way, *Sri Vidya* has the potential energy to purify anything—including the *samskaras* we have accumulated from many births. When one has been initiated into the *Pancha Dashakshari Mantra* and chants it during *Sri Vidya upasana,* this *japa,* combined with meditation, has the power to purify all the impurity within us.

As we proceed with this *sadhana,* all the *chakras* and *granthis,* knots in the subtle body, are stimulated, and the *chakras* are purified from the dust that has clouded them.

---

[8] *Lalitā Sahasranāma,* names 870 and 871

As one goes on doing *mantra japa,* the *chakras* regain their original brightness and glory.

There are many practices in the world. Learned scholars and priests practice many different *mantras*. The Vaishnavas worship Lord Vishnu, and the Shaivites worship Lord Siva. But worshippers of Mother Divine, who are called *Sri Vidya upasakas,* are very few. In *upasana* of Divine Mother, the most important practice is meditation. As long as we are in the external mind, without looking inward, it is not that easy to approach *Sri Vidya*. We need sincerity, intensity and love towards God. As our love towards Divine Mother increases, and we start meditating upon the *mantra* prescribed for *Sri Vidya upasana,* our mind becomes completely controlled and inward. So in *Sri Vidya*, it is said, the aspirant above all needs to be *antara mukha,* inward.

And so the kind of education that one needs for *Sri Vidya* can only be attained by proceeding on the path of meditation. For an ordinary person, it might be a little bit difficult to achieve this inwardness right away. But as all of you are already meditators, it is easy.

The main thing we really need is intense love towards *Sri Vidya.* This will help us attain *antara mukha sthiti,* the state of complete inwardness where the mind comes into total silence. As far as we have the external view, *Sri Vidya* is not that easy. For example, a bee goes in search of flowers in order to get honey, and gathers its pollen from different sources. But finally it reaches the *kamala,* the lotus flower, where it finds what it has been searching for in abundance. In the same way, we have been in this spiritual life in search of the Truth.

Then we come to the place where what we've been looking for is in abundance, we stop and quietly concentrate, totally focusing our attention where we are. That place is *Sri Vidya*. And in this beautiful, forested place of retreat, *Sri Vidya* is in abundance. Here we have the opportunity to experience *antara mukha sthiti,* inwardness, as we proceed in meditation with *mantra japa* and *upasana*.

Shuddha means purity, stainless purity. Meditation is the highest education, because it purifies us and brings us to the state of supreme awareness.

In this world, there are so many different types of education, and different rules go along with each one. In general education, there are innumerable teachers who can teach us all kinds of things. But none of these types of education can truly give us the answer to the question, "What is the world?"

The real teacher is your Self. So wake it up—it is inside, within you. The real education can only be attained through meditation. Because of our *samskaras,* the natures of "I-ness," "me-ness" and "my-ness" are always rising in our heart. It is very important to be mindful of this. So that is why, since the beginning of the world, the *gurus* have been very strict that you wake up at three o'clock to do meditation.

In ancient times, people woke up at three o'clock, *brahmi muhurta,* to start their meditation. Even today, the value of this time, especially from 3:30-4:30 a.m., is considered important. At that hour of the morning, the entire universe is charged with cosmic energy, so it is a very special time. If we meditate consistently during *brahmi muhurta* we will attain *Brahma Jnana;* we experience *Shuddha Vidya,* that is, the purest knowledge, super-Consciousness. People in all walks of life experience these vibrations.

Sri Vidya upasakas from their childhood learned *mantras*. In their *shishya* days—as student disciples—they strictly followed the rules and regulations that were given to them by their *gurus*. The transmission of *Sri Vidya* comes from the *Guru* so we must respect the *Guru*. The *gurus* followed all the rules and regulations, and meditated many years. Their path was so clean that they attained *jnana*. *Jnana* is *vishaya shunyata,* a mind empty of thoughts.

These rules and regulations—which are outlined in the *Patanjali Yoga Sutras, Parashurama Yoga Sutras, Gautama Yoga Sutras*—were followed by the holy *rishis* also. That is why we call them *Patanjali Yoga Sutras, Guru Vashishta Yoga Sutras, Guru Visvamitra Yoga Sutras*—there are innumerable *yoga sutras* named after the holy *rishis*. They gave us so many *yogas* and *sutras*—more than 108 *sutras*. When we look at these *sutras, pranayama,* controlled breathing, *dharana,* one-pointed concentration, *dhyana,* meditation, and all the various *yogas* that lead to salvation, we experience the vibrations that are *Shuddha Brahma Vidya.*

Destiny, generally, is considered to be something beyond our ability to know. What is our destiny? The truth is, our destiny is Realization—the realization of our own supreme Self. Where will we find this destiny? This destiny is within our Self only. So what teachings shall we follow? We need meditation—*Shuddha Vidya*. For *Shuddha Vidya* we need good vibrations. We need good habits: good food habits, less speaking, silence, inwardness—all these things are essential for a spiritual aspirant. Without these attributes, how can we attain the kingdom of spiritual wisdom?

First, we need silence, and only then do we get inwardness. Without that inwardness, if you wake up early in the morning, at three o'clock, and do *yoga* even for one hundred years, it is a mere waste. You need that inwardness. So how can we get that inwardness? Through love towards the Divine. We need that love towards the Divine. You need to trust the Divine. You need to follow strictly the inner One. When your awareness is inside, *Sri*

Vidya says, there is nothing external at all. First you can realize spirituality inside, in your inner world, then you are able to see the same light everywhere in the world.

So *Sri Vidya* starts with that inwardness—*Antara mukha samaradhya*. Otherwise, spirituality is impossible. If your mind is always actively seeking materialistic things, it is not going to achieve the kingdom of the spiritual level. So we need this inwardness. How can we go inward? Whenever we close our eyes, our minds are flooded with innumerable thoughts. So we need to do *pranayama*.

Pranayama controls your thoughts. That is why almost all the *yoga sutras*—those of Parashurama, Bharadvaja, Durvasa, every holy *rishi* who gave beautiful *yoga sutra* teachings—mention *pranayama* to control the thoughts. Whenever you practice *pranayama* before meditation, after five or ten rounds of *pranayama,* your thoughts gradually subside. Your mind becomes so calm and serene, and you are connected with supreme light. So we do *pranayama* to control these thoughts. Gradually and slowly all the thoughts subside and you can do true meditation with intense resolution.

So my dear children, do this sincerely, and undertake the highest education—*Shuddha Vidya.* Stainless purity is the supreme Consciousness. You must experience that blemishless purity inside your heart. If you control your thoughts and purify your heart, billions of suns put together are not equal to the light which is inside in the form of your supreme Self. So in *Shuddha Vidya,* we practice meditation strictly in the morning time every day, regularly, without interruption.

Come to think of it, once when I was meditating in Penusila, a man came and told me, "When I was seven years old, my *Guru* at that time was a magistrate. He took my hand and made me take a vow: 'You must do meditation every day at three o'clock in the morning. Give me your word.' I gave him my word, and to this day I have always kept that vow." How many people respect their *Guru's* words like this? They expect that respect.

And we need that kind of strictness in spirituality. Some days are not good. We are not in wisdom, and we know it; we need some elevation from our low level. Some days we are lazy. We think, "Today I am not feeling well. I will meditate tomorrow when I am a little bit better." So we go one week avoiding meditation. It is very difficult to get the same concentration after a ten day interval. If we keep postponing like that, we will do all other worldly activities except meditation. That is why the *Guru* is so strict about our meditating every day early in the morning.

There are innumerable levels in spirituality. Children, you need to climb all the steps. How many levels? First the root *chakra.* Whenever we are in the root *chakra,* we are always entirely focused on the body. That is why we pray to Ganesha: "O Ganesha! Come out of the root *chakra.* You are in the form of *kundalini*. You are nothing but *kundalini*. You are nothing but *Adi Para Shakti*. You are nothing but the supreme Self. You are nothing but the light! But when the *kundalini* lies asleep in the root *chakra,* it is impossible to advance spiritually, so Ganesha, come out of Your shell. Your grace is very important; then the cooperation from God will come."

When the *kundalini* comes out from the root *chakra,* the *muladhara chakra,* then we forget ourselves. We never think about the body in meditation. We sit three hours, four hours at a stretch in meditation. We never think about the body. We just experience. What do we experience? It is like this: sometimes when we are deeply immersed in our work, you know, we forget everything—even to drink water. We just forget everything when we are seriously at work. We may have wanted so many things—this thing, that thing. But just like that, we forget material things. So when

Ganesha awakens in the root *chakra,* our meditation burns all the negativity in the *muladhara.*

When the *yoga agni* of the *kundalini* rises and travels towards the second *chakra*, we are detached from this world. We never think about this world. All the desires, negative forces and bad *karmas* in the *chakra* are burned in the fire of meditation. That is why we need many sittings of meditation, not just one hour of meditation. Not only here, but after you go home, do all the practices we are doing here, but more than anything else, meditate seriously, even more than here.

So children, seriousness is what we need in our *sadhana.* Remember the honey-bee, searching and searching in the grass flowers, getting its honey in grass flowers, in so many flowers. Honey is really scarce in grass flowers; sometimes there is a little bit. But here, in this lotus flower, there is an abundance of honey. This lotus flower is nothing but *manasa dhyanam*—inner meditation. You can find that supreme light, and you can experience supreme Consciousness. Then there is no more searching for you—you *are* the Supreme! And you begin to experience the *Shuddha Vidya, Sri Vidya.*

So we have wasted forty years, forty-five years, fifty years already. The meaning of our life so far comes to very little. All these years, you have had energy to live, and you are a good person, but now you find it difficult to simply sit. Your mind is turned towards materialistic things. You need to burn all those desires now. For this, you need a strong desire towards spirituality. This doesn't really come under the category of desire. It is a noble desire to want to experience the Divine; this is the reason you are alive. This isn't ordinary desire. There is only one real desire, the divine desire to experience wisdom and inner light. So children, to experience *Sri Vidya,* first entrust yourself to spiritual life. You must practice every day—every day for several hours. We spend too much time talking, and not enough time in silence.

In the olden days, the relationship between the *Guru* and *shishya* was very divine. They treated the *shishya* like their own son; it was very special. Now we do not have opportunities to speak to the *Guru*. Even in India, it is very different than it was before. There is *darshan* and blessings and so on, but not much teaching in the sense of prayer or spirituality. It is important, you know, to speak at least a little bit about spirituality, because people have busy lives, and do not concentrate on spirituality themselves. That's why the *gurus* are not speaking about the Truth. If you are really interested in it, then they also open their hearts. But people are busy and in a hurry, so the *gurus* simply tell them to meditate, do this and do that. We are very unfortunate, we miss all the real spirituality that flavors the Truth.

My children, always have a pure spiritual life inside—*antara mukha samaradhya*—a really spiritual way of life. We need meditation, intense meditation with inner silence. This inner silence comes to us with the practice of *pranayama*. Even if your mind is very disturbed, you can just sit and do *pranayama* five times, ten times, and you will be relaxed and able to meditate, free from any thoughts.

Om asato mā sad gamaya
Tamaso mā jyotir gamaya
Mṛtyor mā amṛtam gamaya

Om śānti śanti śantiḥ

Lokāḥ samastāḥ sukhino bhavantu 3x

ॐ

INQUIRY INTO THE MEANING OF TRUTH

Om Śrī cakra vāsinyai namaḥ
Om Śrī lalitāmbikāyai namaḥ 9x

Śrī vidyām jagatām dhātrīm sṛṣṭi sthiti layeśvarīm
Namāmi lalitām nityām mahā tripura sundarīm 5x

Om śānti śānti śāntiḥ

How did *Sri Vidya* come into existence, and how did people follow it? *Ishwara,* Lord Siva, is the first one who practiced meditation. He was initiated by Mother Divine. This process of meditation dates back to time immemorial. Then the other deities of the Trinity, Lord Brahma and Sri Maha Vishnu, also started meditating. And as Siva, or *Ishwara,* was absorbed in meditation, the *Vedas* arose. Divine Mother dwells always in the heart of *Ishwara.* That is why in one of the *namas,* or names, Mother has been praised as *Kameshwara Brahma Vidya svarupini*. Mother granted the practice of *Brahma Vidya* to *Ishwara,* Lord Siva. So from that time onwards, Lord Siva was absorbed in meditation, and He is the one who taught others the practice of meditation.

Why do people come to spiritual life? According to the *Vedas*, from time immemorial, people have had a question: they have been engaged in self-inquiry. What draws people to follow a spiritual life? It starts when one puts the question to oneself: "Who am I?" In the *Vedas,* this translates into one very simple word: *Koham*. In *vedic* times, many people explored this question, and many of them practiced meditation to find the answer. They taught it to children also.

Koham? Who am I? *Kuta ayanta?* From where have I come? Many people have these questions. Sometimes when we are leading a spiritual life, we also have this question: "We have been born here, and we spend some years on this Earth, and then ultimately everything ends in death. What happens to that individual? The body is left here, but what happens to the soul?" Some people do not believe in the transmigration of the soul. But what happens to us when we die? What happened in the past? Where was I before I was born? From where have I come? Who exactly am I?

These are the questions that arise in the minds of people who have spiritual leanings. They start trying to find the answers. And this inquiry has been continuing since *vedic* times. They are inquiring about a subject that is not common knowledge. And because no one has exact answers to these questions, in order to investigate this subject, an individual or spiritual seeker starts searching for the Truth. And from *vedic* times onwards, this has been a very deep subject. The *Vedas* speak about this: whoever goes deeply into this subject must tenderly take it to heart. Only then can one understand the profound truth given in the *Vedas*.

So Lord Siva, who was created by Mother Herself, was the one who started meditation. He wanted to know what was unknown to Him. And what is unknown? That is the question. We think we know everything. But there is something that is unknown to people. And that unknown is *Satya,* the Truth. It is unknown to us—it was unknown even to Lord Siva at that time. So in order to give this wonderful practice of meditation to all of us, Lord Siva Himself started practicing it. He practiced meditation and He gave it to others. And from that time onwards people began to meditate.

The *Vedas* state very clearly: in the world where we live, we think many of the things around us are real, and that we know everything. But whatever we see with our eyes is not real; it is not the Truth, which is ultimately what we have to look for. The Truth we want is unknown, and to know that unknown—to start the journey to experience that unknown—is why individuals undertake *sadhana.*

Generally, only learned scholars, who are well-versed in the *Vedas,* know how to chant the *vedic mantras.* The meanings are unknown to us. Because we don't understand them, we think that the *Vedas* don't mean anything and have nothing to teach us. Until we know the meaning, we need strong meditation to understand the *Vedas.* As we have been discussing, that which is unknown to us is Truth. And what that Truth is, the *Vedas* explain. The *Vedas* speak only about the Truth and in many, many ways, make us understand what the Truth really is. Very clearly, in one *mantra,* in one *shloka,* the *Vedas* say:

Satyameva īśvare loko
Satya dharma prtiṣṭhitaḥ

Very firmly it states that in this world, *Satya,* Truth, is the one power which creates; it also has the power to sustain and the power of dissolution. *Satya* is the power which can do all three—creation, sustenance and dissolution. Without *Satya,* without the Truth, this universe cannot be controlled at all. And this Truth is indivisible. This Truth has another name: righteousness or *dharma.* And this Truth is also called *Ishwara.* Here *Ishwara* doesn't only mean Siva—the Truth is *Ishwara.* In this way, the *Vedas* go deep into the subject of explaining Truth. We need meditation, at least some hours each day, to understand this Truth.

Another question often asked is: "What is the form of Truth?" Because we have a lot of confusion and differences while speaking about this Truth. In this world there are many paths and many religions. Sometimes when people live in a particular region and follow a particular belief, they think that Truth, or God, is in that particular form only. And people on the other side say that Truth has a different form, a different name.

So what is the form of Truth? Is Truth male or female? This question is also asked often. When Mother comes to the West, people say, "God is always worshipped here as male. But you are bringing the concept of Mother Divine, and Mother Divine is female. So is God male or female?" This question was already asked in the *Vedas* millions of years ago. So when we are speaking about the Truth, we also wonder whether Truth has form—whether it is Ganesha, whether it is *Ishwara,* whether it is Jesus, whether it is light, whether it is this or that.

So people ask, "What is the form of Truth? Is it male or female? And what is the language of Truth?" Sometimes we also wonder, "In what language was Truth given to us? Where does this Truth reside? Where exactly is it? Where is the abode of the Truth?"

The answer is: it is very difficult to grasp the form of Truth. There is no form at all for Truth. In the *Vedas*, it is said, *"Na iti."* This means, "It is not this." We cannot point to a particular form or a particular name or a particular place and say that the Truth is specifically like this, or the Truth is like that, and Truth has this form or that form. On this point, there is a very beautiful *shloka,* or stanza, in the *Vedas,* which says:

Namo brahmane namaste vāyu
Tvameva pratyakṣa brahma vadiṣyāmi
Ṛitam vadiṣyāmi satyam vadiṣyāmi

In this manner, the *Vedas* have given us a message about how to identify the Truth. The *Vedas* say Truth doesn't have a form, it doesn't have a place, it doesn't have a language. So how can we approach the Truth? In this *shloka* it very clearly states that we can see the Truth in the form of the wind, we can see the Truth in the form of fire, we can see the Truth in the vastness of the universe. But we cannot say that Truth only exists in this particular body of water which we have close by; we cannot say that the Truth is within the fire in this particular place; we cannot say that Truth is limited within this boundary of air—because all the *pancha bhutas* are boundless. One cannot capture the Truth and say that it is here only.

The invisible form of Truth is all-pervasive—in all nature, in all the things we see—as the five elements. The Truth that we see in the form of air here is the same that we see in the air anywhere else in the world. Similarly, when we see fire, that same energy that makes things burn is the same in all fire, and that is Truth. In this way, in this unseen way, Truth manifests in different forms, in different places, and it can be called by different names.

So this *shloka* means, "I salute the Creator that is *Brahman. Brahman* is the name we give to the One that has no form. I salute the power in the air. I pay my respects to You, the Truth in all. Realizing that You are the Divine that I see everywhere, I salute You in all things as true Consciousness; I recognize You and salute You as the Truth." That is what the Vedas are saying in this *shloka*.

The process of self-inquiry that began in *vedic* times, which originates in the *Vedas* with the Trinity and all the holy *rishis*, is an ongoing process. This self-inquiry is endless. What is true and what is not true is experienced during the process of this self-inquiry by each particular individual. However much you listen or read in books, Truth must be *experienced* in your own *sadhana*—this is very clearly stated. And this inquiry is endless.

The philosophy of the Vedas and the answers it found in its inquiry into Truth have great significance. They are recognized by spiritual aspirants to be immensely valuable in showing them the way to proceed along this path of inquiry. And so this inquiry continues through the ages in different ways, taking different forms, with different beliefs, in different times. The Bible says Truth is your path. From time immemorial, the Vedas have been discussing this Truth. It is a never-ending process of inquiry. It will always continue.

For meditation, there are three important points. Complete internal freedom is essential. We must be able to think without being influenced by the thoughts of others. The *Vedas* say that in order to think for ourselves, we need total freedom of thought. This is the first point. The second is freedom for *anveshana,* investigation—the freedom to inquire into the inner Being and to ask questions. The third point is self-confidence, or faith in our inner Self. *Bharatiya Dharma Siddhantam,* which lays down the principles of right thinking and conduct according to Indian philosophy, makes these same points.

All people are not the same; they do not think or act alike. And so the *Vedas* do not say, "Only this is the Truth," or "Our God is the only true God," or "There has only been one incarnation of God."

The Bible says, "Truth is your path." From time immemorial, the *Vedas* have been investigating the Truth. They have spoken very clearly about the Truth. They declare that Truth has no name or form, and it is not confined to any particular place. The quest for Truth continues endlessly through the ages. It has not stopped even though we are much more advanced today, and it never will. But the *Vedas* emphasize that we need true internal freedom in choosing our path to Truth. So the three main foundations for spiritual seekers in the quest for Truth are freedom of thought, freedom of inquiry, and complete self-confidence.

The *Vedas* do not say that everyone must follow their teachings. They do not ask us to stick to only one principle or path—they have never said that. The *Vedas* do not try to bind us or confine us within limits. Their vision is very broad and universal. They give us teachings but leave us free to make our own decisions.

The *Vedas* do not say that the Truth is in air or in fire or any other element. They make no such statements. Fire is everywhere in the world; water and air are everywhere, too. The *Vedas* only say that wherever we find these elements, the energy or cause behind them is Truth.

We need this kind of freedom to adopt our own spiritual path to Truth. The *Vedas* recognize the importance of freedom, and that is why they leave us completely free.

We have chosen the subject of Truth and we have been inquiring into it in many ways for many years. Yet we still don't know what Truth is; we cannot define it. So we continue to search endlessly. When the *Vedas* say that Truth is in this or in that, we need to think deeply about these statements and come to our own conclusions. That is what the *Vedas* want us to do. They do not insist that a seeker must go to only one particular place, or follow one particular path to attain the Truth. Since Truth is boundless and all-pervasive, an aspirant can go within himself and find it there! The *Vedas* know this, and that is why they want us to be free to think and decide for ourselves.

When a writer begins to write a novel or story, he creates a character with his imagination. As the story continues, the character grows and evolves until it seems to acquire a personality of its own, independent of the writer. The writer is unable to control its thoughts and actions any more. When the writer sees that character, created by his own mind, grow and mature in this way, he feels very happy.

In the same way, as individuals, we have all the freedom to mold ourselves that the writer has in molding the character in his story. And in the same way that a character grows beyond the writer's ideas, spiritual development takes us beyond all limitations we might have imposed upon ourselves. Once we take up meditation, we are no longer bound by the cage of our body or confined within the limited frame of our mind. The *Vedas* say that no matter how much we might have read or heard about the Truth, we need to expand our awareness through the process of meditation, and experience the light of Truth in our own heart. Our inquiry, in the form of meditation, must continue endlessly—until we actually experience the Truth.

So there can be no question of restrictions at all. When we learn something or get trained in something, sometimes we get stuck there. We must come out of that dead end. When a lot of restrictions are placed on us—that we should only follow a particular path, or only listen to certain things, only read certain things, only do certain things, and so on—our progress comes to a halt. That is why the *Vedas* insist on full freedom for seekers, total wisdom without any restrictions whatsoever. In this way the *anveshana,* inquiry into the Truth, into the Self, can proceed without a stop till the goal of Self-Realization is reached. But without intensity, *anveshana* for the attainment of knowledge of the Truth is meaningless.

Countless spiritual seekers have begun the quest for Truth, and some of them have given it up, causing a break. Many of the religions in this world stopped the practice of inquiry at certain points. They said, "This alone is the Truth." They did not like other prophets and their followers to be considered greater than their own. They felt that their religion was the best and their God the greatest. The teachers of many religions and their followers, too, had very narrow views. Because of this, there was an end to *anveshana*, and they could not progress further.

Time keeps moving rapidly; it moves endlessly every instant like a swift stream. We know that every human being must leave his body one day. The *Vedas* say that *anveshana* must continue without a break, but an interruption comes because of death. So does the inquiry into the Truth stop with death? The *Vedas* tell us that every individual soul is born again, and the inquiry continues in the next birth. So the search for the Self continues endlessly. We do not know in which world it stops.

[Amma laughs] Children, reach the goal in this world, before your next birth!

You are householders, with many complications, problems, negativity and opposition around you in life. It is very difficult for you to meditate at home under these circumstances. You have a lot of problems, I know. But in spite of all these difficulties, continue to meditate, and achieve your goal. As you are in spiritual life, with every breath you *must* continue your efforts. You must not stop your *sadhana,* no matter how much commotion surrounds you.

There are many religions in the world. Many teachers, *Gurus* and incarnations have come to us and taught us in their own way. In *Sanatana Dharma,*[9] when you start the inquiry, you find that there have been innumerable incarnations—Rama, Krishna, Buddha and many others. They were all outstanding personalities, strong in spirit. You can see their divinity. You can see the same divinity in yourself and in me. However, every spiritual aspirant needs to make the inquiry into the supreme Self, the supreme Truth, for himself.

As Amma said before, time keeps moving like a rapid stream. It doesn't stop at all. The life of an individual ends,

---

[9] *Sanātana Dharma*: (*sanātana:* ancient or eternal + *dharma*: the laws of righteousness or moral living and virtue) The ancient laws of righteousness which lay the foundation for leading a truly moral, virtuous life. Their precepts are true for all time.

as we all know, but the inquiry into the Self does not end in one life. You may think that you have been in the spiritual life since the 1960's or 1970's or 1980's, that in this life you were initiated by a *Guru* at a particular time, and then began your *sadhana*. But actually, you did not begin it at that particular time. You began your spiritual journey in a previous birth, and it is continuing in this life also. Make this your last birth, children. [Amma laughs] You should not be born again and again.

This inquiry continues over many lifetimes. That is why we are here. There is no end to this search for the Truth because there is no end to time. Time does not stand still. It keeps moving every instant. We all know that death is the stopping point. But death stops only that particular life and that particular body. It does not stop the ongoing inquiry into the Self, because the Self never dies. The inner being progresses with the inquiry. Death is only a short interval, an intermission, a small break in the play. [Laughter] Once again the individual soul takes a new body and continues its *anveshana* in the next birth.

Shastrajnas, people well-versed in the sacred scriptures, and scientists are constantly carrying on their *anveshana* to unwrap the secrets of the universe. In spite of all their investigations, however, they have not succeeded in learning all the secrets. Will these secrets ever be revealed?

Sri Vidya is *Atma Vidya,* knowledge of the Self. It speaks extensively and profoundly about *Atma anveshana,* the search for the Self, the supreme Being. If we want to acquire the sacred knowledge contained in *Sri Vidya* and understand its secrets, meditation, wisdom and complete freedom of thought are necessary.

With the three freedoms mentioned in the *Vedas*—freedom of thought, through which one develops maturity, freedom of inquiry into the inner Being, and freedom of faith in the Self—we will be able to see and experience that all creation is nothing but Shakti, supreme energy. We will come to know that this Shakti emanates from the *bindu sthana,* the central point in the innermost triangle of the *Sri Chakra,* and it is the root cause of all creation.

Creation is nothing but light and energy; it is divine illumination and power. Shakti is the fundamental principle of creation. When we speak about energy and light at the physical level, we cannot understand them. That is why we inquire into the Self, or the Truth. Knowledge of the Self expands our vision and understanding. The *Vedas* say that a life without the illumination of true knowledge, the *jnana* of *Sri Vidya,* is filled with darkness. *Sri Vidya* is *Maha Vidya,* the greatest knowledge, the greatest education a human being can have.

A spiritual aspirant must have *asakti,* a very intense attraction and desire for God. Without this, progress is impossible and life becomes meaningless. If *daivi prakasha,* divine illumination, is not in our heart, we will remain in darkness forever. *Sri Vidya* speaks about *Atma darshan,* the vision of the soul within. Everyone's vision of the Self or of creation will not be identical. This depends on the *samskaras* of an individual. Everyone in the room will get something different from Amma's lessons. In the same way, each individual's understanding of the Truth will be different. One person might understand it immediately, whereas another might not grasp it even after listening for a long time.

In order to understand and grasp the Truth, *antaranga vikas* and *Atma vikas,* inner expansion and spiritual growth, are needed. The ability to comprehend subtle truths is gained through meditation and ongoing inquiry. It also depends upon the seeker's *samskaras,* as well as his *asakti,* intense longing, for Self-Realization. Discipline in the performance of spiritual practices and the intensity of self-inquiry are absolutely essential. Therefore, Amma once again repeats, every one of you must continue your meditation and *Atma anveshana.* Never stop your *sadhana,* children. Only then will you gradually develop the ability to grasp the Truth.

This Truth, supreme, divine Consciousness, is the *adbhuta karana,* the wonderful cause, of the creation, sustenance and dissolution of the universe. The *pancha bhutas,* the five basic elements of nature, are space, air, fire, water and earth. Nothing can exist without these five elements. Everything in this world depends on them. According to the fundamental principles declared by the *Vedas,* these five elements are themselves alive and contain *shakti*. They have light, and the power even to punish. The *vedic* sages recognized the importance and power of the *pancha bhutas,* so they worshipped them. There are many *shlokas* in the *Vedas* in which salutations are offered to the *pancha bhutas.*

Investigations regarding the five elements continue, but no one has found anything beyond the *pancha bhutas*. Everything in creation consists of the five elements. The *Vedas* say that the *pancha bhutas* have the power to confer grace or inflict punishment on human beings when they are displeased with them. That is why the *Vedas* praise and worship the elements and nature. If we show them disrespect, these elements can get angry and shake the world around us through natural disasters such as earthquakes and floods. Scientists have learned only recently that the five elements of nature have life. The *rishis* of ancient times knew this. That is why it is very clearly said in the *Vedas* that we should protect nature as we would our own beloved mother.

In this modern age, we have been polluting the *pancha bhutas* in countless ways. There is atomic pollution, gas pollution, smoke pollution, water pollution and sound pollution. We ourselves have caused global warming. We are destroying the *pancha bhutas*. That is why so many disasters are occurring in the world, causing untold misery and suffering to human beings. The energies which should be protected have been wasted by us. We need to become aware of the necessity to protect nature and the elements. The *Vedas* had this awareness, and that is why they respected and worshipped nature.

There is a beautiful saying in the *Vedas, Sarvam shaktimayam jagat.* And another equally beautiful one is *Sarvam khalvidam brahma.* What do they mean? *"Sarvam"* means "the entire creation." The whole universe is filled with Shakti, divine Consciousness alone. *Brahma* is another name for that same supreme Consciousness. "*Sarvam khalvidam brahma*" means "All creation is nothing but *Brahma* or *Brahman,* the Absolute."

The sages saw this all-pervasive energy enveloping the universe in their meditation and they began to worship Shakti as Divine Mother. The *rishis* were great beings. They turned their attention inward and enjoyed the blissful state of seeing the light of divine Consciousness within. They did not travel all over the world in search of the Truth that pervades all creation. Closing their eyes, in meditation they saw and experienced the all-pervasive Consciousness and enjoyed the bliss in their own hearts! Then they declared, *"Sarvam shaktimayam jagat!"*

But our present world is entirely different. In the golden era of our ancient times, people had a more broad-minded, universal outlook with consideration for everyone. Now society has changed. We are completely under the influence of "I-ness," "me-ness" and "my-ness." This selfishness is like a strong dose of anesthetic. Before surgery, we are given an anesthetic so that we are not aware of the body being cut open. In the same way, we are so immersed in the anesthesia of thinking only about ourselves that we have no time to think about others, about the Self or about that Consciousness that is all-pervasive.

So that is our problem, and that is why we are unable to comprehend the nature of Truth, the eternal and infinite Consciousness. We cannot experience or enjoy the indescribable bliss of the state of *sarvam shaktimayam jagat*. Only when we stop being so engrossed in our little self can we start the process of inquiry into the eternal Self within and learn to understand its true form.

Sri Vidya very strongly emphasizes *sarvam shakti-mayam. Sarvam* implies *samanatvam,* equality not only among all human beings, but all forms of life. Every being is *samana,* the same. There are no distinctions. All are equal. No one is superior or inferior, high or low. Everyone is *Brahman,* the Absolute. This equality makes no distinction between the rich and the poor. *Samatva* is *dharma,* and applies to all creation. According to *Sri Vidya,* you and I, the tiny ant, all birds and animals, trees, plants and flowers, mountains and rivers, all are pervaded by the same *Shakti*—all are *Brahman.*

We need inner maturity to see and experience such equality. Experience of *samatva* is the result of *paripakva samskaras,* a fully ripened nature developed through several births, leading to an evolved spiritual personality. In our high-tech society we think we have advanced a lot. Having an education doesn't mean we are advanced. Some highly educated people, lacking in inner knowledge and maturity, behave like patients under anesthesia in spite of all their learning. They are under illusion, *maya*. They hurt others and create problems in society.

ॐ

THE SACRED KHADGA MALA STOTRAM

Hridaya Devi Mantra

Sri Vidya gives us the means to overcome this anesthesia, this overpowering *maya.* It gives us the *Khadga Mala.* This powerful *stotra* not only purifies us, it also gives us protection. *Sri Vidya* starts with the *Khadga Mala.*

In *Sri Vidya,* in the *Khadga Mala Stotram,* we worship the *Sri Chakra* and all the energies residing in it. The word *"khadga"* means "sword." The *Khadga Mala* is like a sharp sword which cuts off all our bondages, and destroys all our attachments and vices. *"Mala"* means "garland." So the *Khadga Mala* is a fragrant garland of 176 powerful divine names.

Some people learn the *stotra* by heart and chant it mechanically as they offer a little red *kumkum* powder or a flower at the lotus feet of Divine Mother or to the *Sri Chakra* with the repetition of each name. But one has to understand the meaning behind these sacred names, and do the *puja* with love and devotion, not just repeat the *stotra* mechanically.

The first *mantra* in the *Khadga Mala* is:

Om namo Tripura sundaryai namaḥ

We offer our *namaskaras,* salutations, to the universal energy which resides in the heart *chakra* in the *svarupa,* or form, of *Tripura sundari.* And then the *stotram* speaks about the physical self, its *gunas,* or natures, and the attributes a spiritual aspirant needs to possess. This is the basis from which we begin. Without having a foundation, how can we construct a house? So it is important to start with our own spiritual foundation. We chant:

Hṛdaya devyai namaḥ
We bow down to *Hridaya Devi.*

Hridaya is the place of the heart. What kind of heart? Our heart must be like a seat for nectar, *amrita.* It needs to be a fitting seat for *daivatva,* divinity, completely blemishless. But when we look inside, what is there instead? It is full of *avagunas,* the undesirable *samskaras* of anger, pride, *raga* and *dvesha,* attachment and aversion. If our heart is the seat of *kalmashas,* impure qualities, how can Mother Divine come and sit in our heart? That is why the *Khadga Mala* begins with the heart *chakra,* which has to be completely purified.

Under illusion, *maya,* we have committed so many mistakes in our lives. Every mistake adds to our *karma* load. It is like hitting ourselves with a stone with our own hands. We keep hurting ourselves. Our *gunas* are ruining our life. We wouldn't use a knife or sword to hurt ourselves but we are doing this with our *gunas.* We have suffered so much in this world, and sometimes our lives seem meaningless. With awareness, we come to see that entertaining impurities in the heart causes us to behave in this way—and there is no end to it.

Hridaya devyai namaha means that our heart is the place where *shakti*, the all-pervasive energy of Divine Mother, resides. When we overcome anger and our heart becomes completely free from hatred, pride, jealousy and other negative instincts, divine energy, the all-pervasive Consciousness of Divine Mother, will come and dwell in the *hridaya sthana,* the heart *chakra.* The chanting of the divine *mantra, Hridaya devyai namaha* means all these things.

The *Khadga Mala Stotra* proceeds:

Om namaḥ Hṛdaya devī Śiro devī Sikhā devī
Kavaca devī Netra devī Astra devī….

We recite these *mantras* to illuminate our *chakras*. We must very clearly understand the significance of the first Devi name in the *Khadga Mala—Hridaya Devi.* It does not simply mean that Divine Mother resides in our heart. It indicates that the heart must be pure and sweetened like elixir. Instead, it is poisoned with anger and pride. Why? Because of the effects of the anesthesia of illusion. We must understand that this means we must first of all cleanse our heart.

If every individual had a pure heart filled with nectar, this world would be different; it would not be the way it is. There is so much crime in society today, and many things which should never happen are taking place. But human beings behave the way they do because of their *gunas.* So these negative tendencies in our nature must be completely rooted out. We must look into our heart and question ourselves, "Is my heart full of nectar or its opposite?" If we find any negative qualities in our heart, we must make every effort to overcome them.

We have been ruining our life because we hold on to these negative qualities. We cannot hear what people tell us when they point out our mistakes. We are under the influence of a strong and active anesthetic—the power of *maya,* delusion, has made us unconscious and insensitive. We do not even pay attention to what the *Vedas* tell us.

Chanting of the sacred and powerful name *Hridaya Devi* in the *Khadga Mala* first purifies the heart *chakra,* and then stimulates all the other *chakras*. If the heart is not clean, *Sri Vidya* cannot reside there. The heart is the seat for Consciousness or the Divine. It is said that recitation of the *Khadga Mala Stotra* is not merely an external *puja,* in which the devotee touches the different *chakras* in his body to stimulate them, it is a scientific process. When we say *Hridaya devyai namaha,* we touch the heart *chakra.* Then we touch the crown *chakra* while chanting *Siro devyai namaha,* and after that we touch the medulla oblongata at the back of the head as we say *Sikha devyai namaha. Kavacha devyai namaha* is chanted while touching the hands which protect us, and *Netra devyai namaha,* while touching the eyes. We repeat *Astra devyai namaha* and touch our shoulders. All these places are touched one after the other in this order.

All the energies, as well as the *pancha bhutas* and all the *brahmandas,* the solar systems in the cosmos, revolve eternally around this *shakti,* the energy of the heart place, the *hridaya chakra,* in the form of the luminous *bijakshara Srim*. The *hridaya chakra* must be *amritamaya,* full of nectar. The spiritual journey starts with *Hridaya Devi.* Therefore, we must first clear the heart of all impurities.

Mother Divine, in the *svarupa,* form, of the *Srim bijakshara,* dwells in the heart as *Pranada Prana rupini.*[10] *"Pranada"* is "one who gives life," and *"Prana rupini"* means "the personification of vital energy." This divine energy of *prana* gives life to the *pancha bhutas*, the elements which compose not only human beings, but all creation.

There are several subtle energy centers in the body. When we do *kara nyasa* and *anga nyasa,* we follow a scientific process. In *kara nyasa* we say, *"Angushthabhyam namaha,"* and touch the thumb. Then we say, *"Tarjanibhyam namaha*," and touch the forefinger. In this way we touch each of the five fingers in turn, and then the palm and back of both hands. This is followed by *anga nyasa,* in which different parts of the body are touched in a prescribed order, beginning with the heart.

When we gently touch these places where *chakras* are located, they get stimulated and the knots in the *chakras* are released. That is why *kara nyasa* and *anga nyasa* are

---

[10]*Lalitā Sahasranāma,* names 783, 784.

considered to be an important form of *yoga,* and are done before every *puja*. But even knowing all these things, they will serve no purpose if we remain under the influence of *maya*. We need to clean the heart first; only then can we enter the kingdom of Mother Divine, the blissful realm of *sarvam shaktimayam*. The whole universe is filled with Shakti, and that energy is within you in your heart place!

So *Sri Vidya* begins with this process of cleaning. For us to come and sit in this hall, the place must be clean. If it was not clean, but instead filled with all kinds of things, we would not be able to sit here. In the same way, the *Khadga Mala* begins with the cleansing of the heart *chakra*. The *hridaya chakra* is the seat for supreme Consciousness, for the Divine, praised as *Pranada Prana rupini*. When we are under the influence of *maya,* our heart *chakra* is covered with the dust of illusion. We have to remove this dust from the *hridaya chakra,* so that the divine Shakti, the energy of *prana,* can come and reside there in the luminous form of *Srim*.

Sri Vidya says that all the universes in the cosmos revolve eternally around the *bijakshara Srim*. The heart is the prime place for the supreme subtle energy around which all the other energies of the universe revolve. They are attracted towards that supreme energy which vitalizes the *pancha bhutas,* and they rotate around it in the heart center. Why does this happen? When children are hungry, they run to their mother for food. It is the mother who nourishes them. In the same way, all the energies in the universe derive their energy from the supreme Shakti. That is why they are drawn to that *pranada shakti* like children to their mother and keep revolving around it. And that life-giving, vital *pranada shakti,* the luminous energy of *Srim,* is within our heart!

That is the reason why we speak again and again about the heart as the place where only Divinity, only Mother

Divine, must reside in the form of *Srim*. But in spite of that, our *hridaya chakra* is always enveloped in darkness. It has become the home of negative qualities and impurities. They must be completely removed, children. That is why the *Khadga Mala* begins with the *mantra, Hridaya devyai namaha.* When we touch the heart and repeat this *mantra,* we become aware that our heart needs to be clean and pure so that *tejas,* divine light, can reside there as *Pranada Prana rupini*. This is extremely important for every spiritual seeker.

The life in our body is not merely *tejas,* light. It is also the vital energy that comes from the *pancha bhutas,* without which we could not live or breathe even for one moment. But since this vital force—Divine Mother in the form of *Pranada Prana rupini*— resides in our heart, we do not get energy from the *pancha bhutas,* the *pancha bhutas* get energy from us! Just as the mother feeds and nourishes her children, in the same way, the supreme energy of *prana shakti* within every individual nourishes the five elements! That is why the *pancha bhutas* are always around our body. When the time comes for us to leave this body, the soul departs from the body, and immediately the body, which was very active, becomes motionless, because there is no *prana*. As soon as *prana* departs, the *pancha bhutas* also leave, rendering the body incapable of doing anything, so that it becomes completely lifeless.

Children, our hearts are so filled with commotion, discontent, sorrow, and heavy with *karma* load. What is the solution? When you meditate, all these clouds disappear. Only divine light, elixir remains in your heart *chakra*. Mother Divine always remains in your heart—you can experience Her there. When Mother is inside, there is no unhappiness. Worship of Mother with the chanting of the sacred *Khadga Mala Stotra* is a powerful sword—it cuts all our bondages, destroys innumerable births of our *karma* load, completely purifying the heart *chakra*. It fills us with divine effulgence. We *experience* Mother in our heart and we merge with Her!

The *dhyana shloka* of the *Khadga Mala* declares:

Tādṛśyam khaḍgamāpnoti yena hasta sthitena vai
Aśṭādaśa mahā dvīpa sāmrāṭ bhoktā bhaviṣyati

What this prayer *shloka* says is that the one who holds such a sword in his hand becomes the supreme sovereign who enjoys and rules the eighteen great islands, that is, the whole universe.

Children, *Rig Veda* society was contented and peaceful because they knew Consciousness is in all. All is *Brahma.* Now we want to break the shell of "I-ness" and come out and experience that eternal joy.

Sri Vidya tells us to meditate for eternal life. So meditate more and more. Forget the commotion around you. You are householders, with endless problems and complications of all kinds in your life. You have to face negativity and even opposition from family and friends. Amma knows how difficult it is for you to meditate under such circumstances. Sometimes you are so overwhelmed, you seem to be gasping for one more breath! But you are in spiritual life, so you must continue to meditate more and more—not only at this retreat but also when you go back home.

When you are back in your home, do meditation whenever possible. Mentally be like a sage—like a swan in the mud pond—with a pure heart *chakra* filled with the light of divine Consciousness. That is Amma's wish.

ॐ

ILLUMINE THE INNER SKY

Group Chanting of *Samputitā Śrī Sūktam*

Śrī vidyām jagatām dhātrīm sṛṣṭi sthiti layeśvarīm
Namāmi lalitām nityām mahā tripura sundarīm

Amma's Most Beloved Children,

This morning we discussed the *hridaya* or heart *chakra,* known as the *anahata chakra.* This is the inner heart, which we must make into the seat of the Divine. As long as we have feelings of "I-ness," "me-ness" and "my-ness," it will be impossible for us to come close to God. Only when we are completely free from all feelings of "I, me and mine," can we approach the Almighty. Then our hearts will shine with ever-effulgent divine light.

The question arises, "How can we illumine the *hridaya akasha,* the inner sky of the heart?" Suppose a room has been dark for centuries. The moment we light a lamp in it, the darkness vanishes. There is no place for darkness at all. The darkness in *prakriti,* nature, is dispelled by the radiant rays of the sun. Similarly, the darkness of selfishness, negative *samskaras* and ignorance is removed by the divine light of God's name!

So, children, how is darkness dispelled? A lamp has to be lit. And in order to keep that flame burning, what should we do? We must destroy whatever obstructs that light, such as our ignorance, negativity and the effects of our past *karmas.* This can be achieved through *dhyana,* meditation. When you go inward in meditation, the light of knowledge will begin to glow within your heart so brightly that it will illuminate you and fill the entire world with radiance!

We are alive, but this is not true living. We are truly alive only when we are full of the light of divine knowledge and lead our lives with higher values. At present our lives lack the nectar of *Atma jnana,* knowledge of the Soul—that elixir. In order to attain the radiance of higher knowledge and wisdom, we need *daiva anugraham,* God's grace. And how can we get the blessing of divine grace? It is meditation that gives us a direct connection to God and His grace. The *sadhana* of daily meditation draws God's grace. *Sri Vidya* teaches that it is imperative for a seeker to do regular *sadhana.* When we perform our spiritual practices with discipline, every step we take in life is filled with the fragrance of peace!

It is important to have God's grace for the attainment of any goal in life. An ant cannot climb a mountain and reach the peak by its own efforts. But with *daiva anugraham* even a tiny ant can do so! There is a story in which it is said that an eagle carried the sun in its beak. Is that possible? Anything is possible when we have the grace and blessings of Divinity! Each and every step of our life will be divinized when we have God's grace.

Actually, many people in this world have achieved unimaginably great things. They think that their achievements are due to their own efforts and abilities. They are elated because they think that they have gained knowledge or understanding by their own efforts. But we should not forget that God's grace is behind our every effort. Without divine grace we cannot move an inch. That which makes us understand anything, or achieve anything, is divine grace alone. Never forget, children, that the hand of God's grace is behind every effort we make. Without that grace, we cannot move even our little finger! Our life is itself the greatest blessing and we have it only because of

God's grace. Knowing that God's grace is behind every move or effort we make, that itself is a great blessing. That is why the *Vedas* declare:

> *Sarvam tejomayam sarvam kāntimayam*
> *Sarvam śakti mayam*
>
> Everything is glowing with divine radiance
> Everything is full of divine energy.

At the moment, we are unable to see that everything is shining brilliantly with divine effulgence. Why are we not able to do so? To see the light of Divinity in all things, our heart must become pure as crystal. This is made clear in the opening *mantras* of the *Khadga Mala Stotram.* The first prerequisite in spirituality is that our heart must be completely without blemish. So when we chant:

> *Om Aim hrīm srīm aim klīm sauḥ*
> *Om Hṛdaya devī*

we are praying for the purification of the *hridaya sthana,* the heart *chakra.* We are asking God to fill our heart with true humanity. Only then can we reach the level of Divinity. When our heart is impure, we cannot reflect the effulgence of divine knowledge.

We need to give up all our wicked and obstinate traits such as hatred, jealousy, envy, selfishness and negative thoughts. Every selfish thought needs to be rooted out of the heart completely and replaced with devotion and compassion. That is the kind of heart we need. Negative qualities are like black curtains which prevent us from coming close to God. We cannot move even one foot towards God because of the heavy layers of negativity within.

It is only when our heart is completely purified that we can ascend step by step—first into true humanity, and then into Divinity. At that moment we will spontaneously exclaim,

Sarvam khalvidam Brahma
Everything is verily Brahman!

So, if one does *puja* mechanically without first purifying the heart *chakra*, it may give some benefit, but will not bring the expected result.

Why are there so many differences and disturbances in this world? Why talk about the world? Even in the home, two people cannot live in peace with each other! They can't understand each other or work together in harmony. Sometimes we feel that the other person is doing things wrong, and that is why there is so much commotion in the family. But each individual has his or her own viewpoint, and it is because of these differences in attitude and behavior that disturbances are created. The commotion in the family is carried over into society.

That is the root cause for most of the problems we have today in society. Every individual is not a saint. Therefore, due to the impurities in the hearts of the people, which are caused by their different *samskaras*, disharmony arises in every sphere of life. In order to remove these differences and disturbances, it is not enough to be a spiritual aspirant; it is not sufficient to listen to discourses, or even to spend some time in meditation. We need to know and understand what the real problem is, where it lies, and what we can do to rectify it. The solution lies in making our heart pure as crystal—completely stainless and without blemish.

The impurities in our hearts make it impossible for us to understand others. We think we are right, but others feel that they are right. This naturally creates differences of opinion, which begin in our homes. It is extremely important to understand this point with an open mind and heart. Ask yourself, "What is causing this obstruction? Why am I unable to succeed in my *sadhana*?" The cause is nowhere but within yourself. For many births we are trapped in this negativity. It is in your own hands to remove the obstruction and solve the problem. The solution is: purify the *hridaya sthana*, the heart *chakra*. You cannot be closer to the Divine than in the *hridaya sthana*. Once the heart is completely pure, free from the entanglements of negativity, all the sufferings you have endured for years—and through countless births—will vanish forever!

There are many *Vedas* and other scriptures which describe different methods for the practice of meditation. In the olden days, one of the spiritual leaders, known as Shankaracharya, the head of a *pitha* or holy center of worship, said that women should not chant the *Vedas*, as they were not eligible to do so. This happened about 150 years ago.

This caused a great upheaval. All the women gathered together and strongly opposed the opinion of the Shankaracharya. They said that the *Vedas* were full of the light of *jnana*, true knowledge. Many of the *Upanishads* and scriptures had originated from women. There had been many women saints, sublime souls who had blessed the world by their wonderful knowledge. The women argued these points.

Actually, *Sri Vidya rupa* is *akhanda*: the form of *Sri Vidya* is eternal, indivisible and indestructible. It is neither male nor female. Blissful, supreme Consciousness has taken the name of *Sri Vidya*! *Sri Vidya* has manifested on Earth to impart the highest knowledge to all. *Sri Vidya* is divine light, which pervades all the universes, surrounding and enriching them with its radiance. No one has the power or ability to control this supreme light. No one can say that only one particular group of people can come under its illumination and be bathed in its divine effulgence.

Everyone has the right to be illumined by the glow of this supreme light. So there is no restriction at all regarding the practice of *Sri Vidya*—both men and women have an equal right to this divine knowledge.

Sri Vidya is *antah richas*—a very beautiful expression meaning "inner effulgence." *Sri Vidya* is inner light, which is in each and every individual, in every living being. A call has come to all of you to know and realize this *richas*, this effulgence! Just imagine what has brought you here. This is not the call of an ordinary person—it is a divine call! A divine force has brought all of you here. It has been said in the *Vedas* that one should spend some time doing *sadhana* in a very remote, forested area. They also say that it would be ideal to meditate at the foot of the hills. And here you are all meditating in a forest at the foot of the Garudadri Hills! All this has happened not by your will, but by the will of the Divine. A divine force is behind all that is taking place here.

All of you have come here from far-off places—from different parts of the world. Some of you have crossed oceans to come to this very remote forest. Just think for a moment about what is happening here. The way you are living here is very different from your normal lifestyle at home. True, there are facilities here for sleeping and eating, yet everything is different from what you are accustomed to. All this has happened according to divine will. Some unknown force is waking you up early in the morning and making you sit for meditation. You are like instruments in the hands of God.

Children, you are both fortunate and blessed to become instruments in the hands of God! You should consider yourselves to be the greatest and luckiest among all people, because in your lifetime you are spending at least a few hours, a few days, in searching for the supreme light!

In this world, in our ordinary life we have to climb step by step in order to reach the highest level—for example, to attain the position of the president. Even one who attains that position can represent only his or her own country, not the whole world. But we are in search of that Divinity who is the president or supreme sovereign of the entire universe! That Divinity is *Sri Vidya*—supreme Consciousness. That is the deity we are trying to approach in the form of *Sri Vidya*. The form of *Sri Vidya* is *akhanda chid rupa*—indivisible, indestructible and supremely blissful awareness! We do not know it, but that form is within each and every one of us as divine light. That is what we are trying to approach and realize, and for that, the first step is complete purity of heart.

Beyond this world, there are *brahmandas,* universes, and planets, galaxies and stars. Some energy is working behind the entire cosmos, and the *rishis* call that energy *Sri Vidya*. *"Sri"* is *aishvarya,* boundless treasure. When we practice meditation, we attain the highest knowledge, and our heart becomes so pure that we are able to experience the divine light within. This is *Sri Vidya*. Of course, repetition of the *Pancha Dashakshari Mantra,* the fifteen-syllable *mantra* sacred to Devi, chanting of *Sri Lalita Sahasranama* and *Sri Chakra puja* are included in *Sri Vidya.* But meditation and inner purification, that is, complete purity of the heart *chakra,* are the most important aspects of *Sri Vidya*.

Let us take the next *mantra* in the *Khadga Mala: Siro Devi. "Siras"* means "head." The lotus of a thousand petals, the inner universal lotus, is situated at the crown of the head. But what about the mind? Our mind is full of countless worldly thoughts.

In the past, when people came to India from Afghanistan and other places, they crossed the Sindhu River. They could not pronounce the sound, *si,* in Sindhu, so they said *hi* instead. That is how the word *Hindu* originated from the name of the Sindhu River, and how the people living in India came to be called *Hindus*. This word, "Hindu," does not exist in the *Vedas*. The *Vedas* are eternal light. This light is for everyone. The great *rishis,* who gave us the sacred *Vedas,* do not say anything at all about religion. Their vision is very wide. Their blessings are for the entire world. A *rishi* is not like a physical person. He himself is the Light. Wherever he travels in society, he causes a revolution. Yesterday we talked about divine energy, which resides in the heart lotus of all beings, as *Pranada Prana rupini.* The great sages knew that this energy is the same in everyone. That is why they prayed, "Let the people of the entire universe be always in happiness, joy and peace."

In *Sri Vidya,* or *Atma Vidya*, the knowledge of the Soul, when we talk of the blessings of the holy *rishis,* we are not referring to any particular individuals. The views of the *rishis* are luminous with open-mindedness. Their words are a revolution against the narrow ideas and negative attitudes of people like the Shankaracharya. We respect the *pithadhipati,*[11] the Shankaracharya, but we do not agree with his views.

"With all due respect," said the ladies, "we have the right to chant the *Vedas* because of their wonderful teachings." Meditation and *tapas* are very difficult to perform. Even listening to spiritual discourses is not easy. We have a great deal of darkness in our society and also in our homes. We are full of ignorance. But we know that meditation is the highest *sadhana,* so we love and respect meditation. We worship *tapas,* and feel impelled to practice it.

---

[11] *pithādhipati:* Head of a religious or monastic institution. Not to be confused with Ādi Shankarācharya, the great and open-minded sage who revived *Sānatana Dharma.*

If it is God's will, then alone will we be able to meditate. We may try to meditate, but if it is not Mother's will, we will never be able to do so. Only with the grace of Mother Divine is it possible for us to close our eyes and go into meditation. Gradually, our hearts will become completely pure and stainless. Then we will see the light of Divinity in our own heart, as well as in the entire universe. The *rishis* who have experienced it say that it is a very special light. The words of the holy *rishis* come from the Truth—they come from the divine, supreme Consciousness Itself!

My dear children, Amma expects more and more intensity in your *sadhana*—not only here at the retreat, but throughout your entire life. Have that divine thirst and hunger towards Mother and realize the Divine. Reach your destination, and share your love and the light of your divine knowledge with everyone. Illumine the entire cosmos! This light is within each and every one of you, but it is covered by ignorance. This is because of lack of maturity. You need the grace of the Divine to see and experience that divine light within yourself.

In meditation, be more in tune with spirituality, and experience more and more love for all beings. Love everyone. Remove every trace of selfishness and negativity from your heart, and meditate well. Try to see God in everyone.

* * * * *

Tomorrow we will talk about *Siro Devi.* At the beginning of a *puja,* we usually do *anga nyasam*. This is when different parts of the body are reverently touched and divine energy invoked into them. In the *Khadga Mala,* in the very first *mantra,* Devi is specifically called *Hridaya Devi,* one who resides in the heart *chakra.* In the second *mantra,* She is addressed as *Siro Devi,* in the third as *Sikha Devi,* and in the fourth and fifth, She is called *Kavacha Devi* and *Netra Devi.* All these *mantras* are universal energies, universal powers residing in the *Sri Chakra.*

The *Sri Chakra* itself emerges from the *bindu sthana.*[12] It is a symbol of the entire universe, but the universe is like a tiny atom in the *Sri Chakra!* So when we worship the *Sri Chakra,* we are really adoring the entire universe in the form of a geometric diagram or a three-dimensional *meru.*[13] So far we have talked about the energy of Consciousness. We worship that Consciousness, and that Consciousness is nothing but our own supreme Self!

The *Vedas* recognize the value of nature. Without the trees, mountains and water, one cannot survive here on this Earth. They say that there is a lot of feeling in nature. That is why the *rishis* began showing their respect and expressing their gratitude to nature. They started worshipping trees, such as the *pipal* and *banyan.* The *banyan* is a huge tree that can branch out over miles! The ancient sages respected, worshipped and showed their gratitude to the energy, the power behind trees. They were aware that if they cut the trees down, there would be less life-sustaining oxygen, and no rainfall at the right time.

They prayed not only to trees, but also to the mountains and rivers. It is said in the *Vedas* that in its lifetime a tree serves us in many ways—it offers us its leaves, flowers and fruit, it gives us shade and also provides us with oxygen. A tree is very useful to humankind. Compared to the service a

---

[12]*bindu sthāna, bindu:* A point inside the main triangle of the *Sri Chakra.* The highest point on the *Sri Chakra meru.*

[13] *meru:* Three dimensional representation of the *Sri Chakra* in crystal, silver, gold or pancha dhatu, an alloy of five metals. It is shaped like a four-sided pyramid, and incorporates all the nine enclosures of the *Sri Chakra.*

tree gives, the *Vedas* say, a human being does nothing! [Laughter] That is why the *rishis* felt grateful to trees, and showed their feelings by praising and worshipping them. They knew that not only do trees promote good health by providing oxygen and purifying the atmosphere, the bark and leaves of many trees have medicinal properties. Trees also bring good seasonal rains. But now we have spoiled everything. We have been ruining nature by polluting it in so many ways, and we are losing all the treasures with which nature has blessed us.

The *rishis* are the pillars that hold *dharma*, truth and righteousness on their shoulders. Without *dharma*, without truth, without righteousness, it is impossible to sustain humankind. So we need at least a little bit of *dharma* in our society. We need to think of others, of their happiness, health and progress. If everyone thinks only about himself, what will happen to society? If your every thought is for yourself alone, and if everyone thinks, "I will do what I want," then the entire society will be ruined by the pollution of such a selfish and negative attitude.

When we talk about the holy *rishis,* we are not simply referring to good persons. A holy *rishi* does not mean an individual with a physical body. It means divine effulgence—that is what a *rishi* really is! The *rishis* had realized that they were not the body, mind or intellect. They had experienced the Truth. Their words brought about a transformation in society because they came directly from the Truth. That is the greatness of the holy sages. Their words are the purest divine nectar of true knowledge. That is why we are still following the teachings of the ancient sages.

Some tradition-minded people are unhappy that we are chanting the *Gayatri Mantra,* and the *Mrityunjaya Mantra* for the sick. It is a healing *mantra*. It heals the body, it cleans the trees, it cleans all nature. It cleans the *pancha bhutas,* the five elements. It even heals the sun and the moon! We have the whole circle of true knowledge in our bodies—the sun here, the moon here, fire here. [Amma points to the left eye (moon), the right eye (sun) and the *ajna chakra,* the place between the eyebrows (fire).] So whenever we chant these *mantras,* their healing vibrations slowly enter into the atmosphere and purify the whole environment. They clean the entire world and the whole universe. But some people are unhappy. What can we do? [Laughter]

We know from experience that when we chant *mantras* we feel peaceful and relaxed. If we chant them in the correct way one hundred times, we get one hundred percent peace and relaxation. The *Samputita Sri Suktam* is so beautiful and powerful.

[The session ends with the chanting of *Om* nine times.]

ॐ

SRI VIDYA DISPELS THE DARKNESS OF IGNORANCE

Śrī vidyām jagatām dhātrīm sṛṣṭi sthiti layeśvarīm
Namāmi lalitām nityām mahā tripura sundarīm

Yā devī sarva bhūteṣu śakti rūpeṇa samsthitā
Namastasyai namastasyai namastasyai namo namaḥ

Embodiments of Divine Soul, Amma's Most Beloved Children,

When did the practice of *Sri Vidya upasana*—the worship of Divinity in the form of *Sri Vidya*—begin, and what was its origin? It is *ananta*—it has neither beginning nor end. Nobody knows when it really started. It has existed from time immemorial. Lord Siva Himself performed it, and then the other two deities of the Trinity—Lord Brahma and Maha Vishnu—followed. Later, all the *rishis* began to practice *Sri Vidya upasana*. A *rishi* is a seer, one who sees the Truth. Speaking about the *rishis,* it was pointed out yesterday that when we refer to the *rishis,* we do not mean any particular individual. The *rishis* were broad-minded revolutionaries who, from time to time, brought about a transformation in society when it seemed to be drowning in the darkness of ignorance.

During such times, the *rishis* traveled far and wide. They met people personally and revealed to them the secrets of the *Vedas* and other sacred texts. In this way they brought about a wonderful transformation in the thinking of the people. In recent times, one such *rishi* was Dayananda

Saraswati,[14] whose greatness was recognized by Swami Vivekananda.[15] Dayananda Saraswati was undoubtedly a truly revolutionary social reformer. During his time, the people were confused regarding the true precepts of *dharma,* because various teachers of philosophy had been giving wrong messages to the people. So he went from place to place and met people. He made them aware of *satya*, Truth, as taught in the *Vedas,* and removed their confusion.

We cannot recognize *rishis* simply by looking at them. We can know them by the light of their teachings and their actions. Whatever we are learning now, and what we read in the *Vedas* and ancient scriptures or in the commentaries on them, comes to us from the holy *rishis.* Even though they are not with us physically, we can feel their presence through their words of eternal wisdom. They have left us a truly invaluable treasure.

We all know that *Kali yuga* is the age of darkness and ignorance. But *Sri Vidya*—which is praised as *Atma Vidya,* knowledge of the Self—says that no matter how much ignorance there may be in any age, *bhakti,* love for God, will never die. It will live forever. The faith that people have in their hearts will not diminish, and the intensity of their interest in spirituality will not wane.

When the sun rises, there is day, and when it sets, we have night. In the *Vedas,* night has been compared to a rock. Why was it likened it to a rock? Night has no light, and light cannot penetrate into a rock. In spirituality, darkness stands for ignorance. That is why the scriptures compare the heart unreceptive to the teachings of Truth to a

---

[14] Dayananda Saraswati (1824–83): Indian religious reformer, founder of the Arya Samaj movement.

[15] Swami Vivekananda (1863-1902): Most well-known disciple of Sri Ramakrishna Paramahamsa.

dark night, or a hard rock. Some people can listen to a beautiful *bhajan* or watch a sacred *puja* and remain completely untouched and unmoved. The hearts of such people are said to be like the night, or a rock. People with such hearts have no understanding of the precepts of the holy scriptures.

But what happens to night? Even though it is dark and appears to be as impenetrable as a rock, as soon as the sun's rays appear at dawn, all the darkness vanishes! Meditation is like the morning sunrise—it fills our lives with light. It gives us awareness, it inspires us and gives us calmness, happiness and peace. Such is the power of meditation, filling us with divine light and making our hearts very soft.

The very word *"Sri"* means "radiance." So *Sri Vidya* is the effulgence of supreme wisdom. *Sri Vidya* does not want anyone to remain in darkness. It wants to fill every individual with the light of knowledge. It wants to remove the darkness of ignorance from every heart, transforming the darkness of night into the light of day!

We have been inspired by countless holy people. From time immemorial, the ancient *rishis* performed rigorous *tapas.* Like camphor, they sacrificed themselves in the blazing flame of *yoga* and attained Self-Realization. They *saw* that supreme light—they *became* that light! And then they dedicated their lives to spreading that light to all humanity. They wanted us to experience that light also, and visualize it within us. This *jyoti,* light, is indestructible and ever-burning.

Actually, no matter how diseased the body may become, the light within never diminishes. Every particle of the cosmos has the same energy, for the source of everything is universal light alone. When that universal energy undergoes *vikara,* or change, it takes many forms. It is due to *vikara* that innumerable *sakaras,* or forms, emerge from the same supreme energy. That is how creation began and how all creatures came into being. All the diverse forms we see in the world—insects, reptiles, animals and human beings—are pervaded by the same universal light. The light which illumines the universe shines in every being on this Earth.

Embodiments of Divine Soul, Amma's most beloved children, the *rishis* wanted to uplift the society to the highest level of consciousness. What we see is changing and changing and changing. But the light inside is indestructible and eternal. Our heart is like a stone. It has no feeling for helping people. We have materialistic desires inside. *Sri Vidya* opens our hearts. When we chant *Hridaya Devi,* we are telling Divine Mother: "My heart is Your seat. But it has all these worldly desires and negativities. Remove these, clean my heart and let me experience the light, the Truth. You are always here, already in my heart. Let me experience You." Open your *hridaya akasha,* the inner sky within you, children. Burn all your *karma* load with meditation. Burn the billions and billions of births of the worst, heinous *karma* load!

Sri Vidya goes back to time immemorial. It starts with Lord Siva. Dayananda Saraswati inspired the ordinary people. He said the *Vedas* were for everyone, even women. So many became meditators and *Brahma jnanis.* Amma wants to see you do the same. Children, travel in the world. Give light to everyone.

ॐ

SIRO DEVI: DIVINITY OF THE SAHASRARA

Embodiments of Divine Soul, Amma's Most Beloved Children,

[Amma shows a picture of the *Sri Chakra,* and points to the point in the middle.]

Gazillions and gazillions of universes come from that one *bindu* point. The palaces of the *Sri Chakra* have many enclosures. To reach the c enter of Mother Divine, one has to cross these enclosures. Without crossing the 16 *avasthas* one cannot get Self-Realization.

Siro is the crown *chakra,* the *sahasrara,* at the top of the head. It is also called the *avyakta sthana* or *chakra*—the *chakra* which is unseen, invisible. It is the *shakti sthana,* the place where Shakti resides. This is where *maya,* illusion, is born, and knowledge, too. It is also the *laya sthana,* the place of dissolution where everything merges with universal energy and disappears.

Chanting the *mantra* "*Siro Devi*" causes all thoughts to subside and completely roots them out. When the *siro bhaga*—the crown *chakra*—is completely freed from delusion, then we will be free. The *Khadga Mala* has the power to burn away all thoughts. The mind—*chitta*—is the source of thoughts. It is the seat of the brain. We are completely entertained by worldly things. The 180 names or *mantras* in the *Khadga Mala* have the power to burn all these thoughts away. Regular practice of meditation burns away all these thoughts. Then the *aham,* ego, is not there at all and one is free.

The Almighty or supreme Consciousness—whatever name we may call it—is nothing but that effulgence. It is indivisible; it cannot be divided. But we have manifested as its sparks. Since this division has been made in something which is indivisible, we have entered into *maya* and are suffering in this world. *Tapas* is the one way for this divided light to merge back into that indivisible energy and light. *Tapas* is what unites the individual self with the universal Self. What is *tapas?* It is the effort we make, the austerity or meditation we do to merge with the Divine.

This beautiful art was given to humanity by the *Vedas.* They say:

Sarvam shaktimayam jagat: The whole universe is filled with the energy of the Divine.

How is it possible to understand this? When the universe was formed, there was only *nirakara Brahman,* the formless supreme Consciousness, or Consciousness without attributes. It became *akara,* with form, and assumed the myriad forms we see in the universe. The same energy, the same light, is present in each and every atom of this world. This effulgence was distributed to every particle of the universe equally—planets, stars, creatures of all types such as reptiles, insects, animals, human beings. So there is nothing about which we can say, "This is not God, this is not the Almighty, this is not the Supreme," for everything in the cosmos, without exception, is a manifestation of the Divine!

The *Vedas* start with the declaration:

Sarvam khalvidam Brahma:
Everything is verily Brahma!

They clarify the whole subject in the introduction itself. The holy *rishis* who gave us the *Vedas* did not make these statements lightly—they actually *experienced* them. They knew that all creation is filled with one supreme energy only!

Children, when you open the *Rig Veda*, the first beautiful saying is:

(An)Īśwara anirvacaniyam divya prema svarupa

"Divya" means "divine;" *"prema"* means "love." *Iswara* always has a loving nature. Everything in nature—mountains, trees, flowers—is so beautiful, but we never find anything that cares so much about us anywhere in the world as *Iswara. (An)Iswara,* the Almighty, the divine Father and Mother, is everywhere, ever with everybody, all the time, under all circumstances, with love like a full moon. The full moon looks so beautiful, milky white in color, with a little lemon and gold. Moonlight is not completely white—when you mix all these colors you get the color of the moon. Billions and billions of moons put together is not equal to a glimpse of the Divine Almighty, who shines with love, only love, towards Her kids. *Anirvachaniyam*—it is very difficult to define this love in any language.

But what if your body has made mistakes? Doesn't *Iswara* care about that? What if your personality is unpleasant sometimes?

You are not a person. Spirituality never agrees with that word. You are not a person— you are *Brahman*. You are the supreme *Brahman*! Your Self is that One. But what about my mistakes, you might say. This is like saying, "Oh dear, there are clouds in the sky." Children, you are the sky and not the cloud. In front of the Meru Mountain, the pebble is nothing. It is not visible. So even if you make mistakes, knowingly or unknowingly, Divine Mother or Divine Father will never find fault with their children. Divine Mother always has more and more love towards Her children—only love.

ॐ

SRI KHADGA MALA — WAVES OF EFFULGENCE

The literal meaning of the name *Khadga Mala* is "sword" plus "garland." *Khadga* is *kanti*, radiance, effulgence. *Mala* is curves, strands, waves of that effulgence. When we put these two words together, what do we get? The names of the energies in the *Sri Chakra*. They are like waves and curves around the *Sri Yantra,* in the middle of which is the *chintamani griha,* the place of the wish-fulfilling gem. The *Khadga Mala* is *shakti,* a powerful divine radiance, more powerful than a laser beam—millions and billions of times more powerful than a laser beam. We all know that a laser can burn anything. The energy of universal Consciousness permeates each and every particle of this creation—not an atom is excluded. Everything is saturated with the same energy and light—and that light is nothing but the effulgence of Divine Mother!

The names in the *Khadga Mala Stotra* extolling the supreme Goddess are not ordinary names. They are powerful *mantras*—they are *kanti chaitanya rupa*, effulgent embodiments of divine awareness. They are one with that conscious light, *prathama kanti*. The names do not represent physical forms; they are the subtle forms of different aspects of Shakti, with names such as *Siro Devi, Sikha Devi, Kavacha Devi, Netra Devi* and so on. They are all forms of the one supreme Consciousness alone. The ancient *rishis* saw these forms; they were drenched in their incredible *kanti,* light. The *Khadga Mala* is a beautiful garland of names extolling the one supreme light!

The *Khadga Mala* is an exquisite garland of praise offered to that Consciousness which fills and surrounds the entire universe. And the whole universe has been pictured in this chart of the *Sri Chakra*. It shows us the artist's concept of the different enclosures, which are nothing but aspects of supreme Consciousness.

The *Sri Chakra,* with all its enclosures and arrangements of triangles and *padmas,* or lotuses, is nothing but the subtle form of *kanti,* the radiance of divine effulgence. This *Khadga Mala* is like a sword of light, millions and millions of times more powerful than a laser beam. It is extremely sharp, and there is nothing in this world it cannot cut.

The *siro bhaga,* which is the area of the brain, is the seat of the mind, which is full of innumerable thoughts. We are influenced by countless material things and get entangled in the endless web of thoughts. How can we escape from this web? Though we have been practicing meditation, and though we are leading a spiritual life, our thoughts never cease. That is why we need to chant the sacred *Khadga Mala Stotra.* When we recite the names of supreme Consciousness in this divine s*totra,* the vibrations of the *bijaksharas* in the *mantras* have the power to destroy all the thoughts seething in our brain. The *Khadga Mala* is the sword of divine light! It is extremely sharp—sharper than anything in the world. It can cut our most deep-seated thoughts from their very roots.

We have come into this world from *Para Brahma,* supreme Consciousness, eternal divine effulgence. From the highest realm we have come down to this Earth. Now from this low place, we need to ascend once again to the top. Coming down, or descending, is called *avarohana,* and ascending, moving upward, is known as *arohana.* So from the highest peak, the top, we have come to the bottom, and from here we must return to the heights from which we came. From *Nirakara,* the formless *Para Brahma,* we have become *akara,* with form—from the boundless we have become limited. Now, from this form, we need to return to the formless state. That is what the *Khadga Mala* teaches us, and that is what it helps us achieve, because it is nothing but the embodiment of *nirakara*—supreme energy!

As you practice meditation—and some of you have been meditating regularly for a number of years—sometimes you get disturbed in the middle of your *sadhana*. Negativity enters the mind; you are overcome by depression; and at times you may even fall into inertia. These things happen to meditators during the course of their *sadhana*.

But you should never give up *dhyana*. Meditation is the right path, meditation is the supreme path, for it burns to ashes all of our thoughts and *samskaras*. We can free ourselves from thoughts through *dhyana*. The regular practice of meditation purifies us and makes us glow with divine radiance. It frees us from all our bondages and takes us to the *nirakara* state.

As we continue to meditate, as we progress in our *sadhana,* all the negativities in our mind, all our depression and all the other inner impurities begin to evaporate in the heat of *dhyanagni,* the fire of meditation. These benefits may not be visible outwardly. And during the period when all our impurities are being burned, we may sometimes face problems such as depression, restlessness created by too many thoughts, and even inertia. These things happen to *sadhakas* during the process of inner purification through meditation.

Never give up, never lose hope, but continue with your *sadhana,* for you have chosen the right path. Meditate regularly, and as you progress, you will surely achieve your final goal in this very lifetime. Then you will be in complete *shanti,* and the *siro chakra* will become totally thought-free.

ॐ

POWER OF THE BIJAKSHARA "AIM"

Amma will now tell you a true story about Kalidasa. It is an inspiring tale which reveals how he was before he received divine grace, and how he was transformed by it.

Kaliya was a very ordinary boy. He was a dullard—illiterate, very innocent and ignorant. He knew nothing. He was a simple cowherd, who took cows out to graze. That was all he could do. Even though people tried to teach him things, he was unable to understand anything. He would make mistakes and do things wrong. That was his nature.

He often called out to his mother, *"Ai, ai!"* The word *"ai"* means "mother" in Sanskrit. By ignorantly repeating the incomplete *bijakshara Aim* sacred to Divine Mother, he was graced by the full power of that *bijakshara!* The *Aim bijakshara* is extremely powerful. Its repetition removed all the ignorance and dullness in Kalidasa. His mind was filled with cosmic light and energy, and in that supreme light he saw the cosmic form of Mother Divine shining before him! He was completely transformed. He began to compose *shlokas* and *stotras* spontaneously! He became famous as a king among poets, and wrote many great plays and immortal poems. He was respected for his wisdom and honored as a great person of his time. It is true that by chanting just one *bijakshara* he was showered with divine grace. He was greatly blessed, and the ignorant and illiterate Kaliya became the renowned Kavi Kalidasa, the great poet Kalidasa!

All this actually happened. Kaliya, the young Kalidasa, was very ignorant, but he was completely transformed by the power of just one *bijakshara!* We may not be ignorant like Kaliya, but our minds are full of countless worldly thoughts, and we are completely under the spell of *maya,* delusion. Yet we have a chance—there is hope. If we practice regular *sadhana,* meditating sincerely with intense concentration, we too can be transformed like Kalidasa. That is why Amma has told you this story—to inspire you to continue your *sadhana* with faith and enthusiasm.

Meditation is nothing but effulgent light. When we are completely under the influence of the mind, the brain acts according to the whims of the mind, and we are thrown into total darkness. This is called *avidya,* ignorance. We are in complete darkness. But when we meditate, all the darkness of ignorance is dispelled because meditation itself is light. This light penetrates into our brain system and burns away the mind, which is the cause of all the problems in this world. Meditation is like a powerful beam of laser light that penetrates into our brain system and fills the ever-active mind with light and peace. Children, do not permit the mind to rule your thoughts and actions. Let the *buddhi,* the intellect, be your guide. Your mind will be filled with the light of wisdom when you meditate. That is why meditation is so important for spiritual seekers.

Kavi Kalidasa became not only a king among poets, he also became a king of *Sri Vidya.* He became one of the enlightened practitioners of *Sri Vidya*. The grace and blessing he received by chanting the *Aim bijakshara* inspired him to take up *Sri Vidya upasana.* He gave great importance to the *Aim bijakshara* because that was the one he had repeated. Such is the amazing power of this sacred seed letter!

In some of the *Upanishads,* the power of the *bijaksharas,* including *Aim,* has been discussed very extensively. The *Upanishads* say that when a seeker meditates on these seed letters, especially on *Aim,* the darkness in him is replaced with eternal light. We are now in ignorance, but all this darkness will be completely dispelled when we chant the sacred *bijaksharas*. The *Aim bijakshara* brings *tejas,* divine light, and the whole *siro* region, the *sahasrara,* is flooded with *tejas* when we chant *Aim*. All our ignorance vanishes forever!

At present we are sunk in darkness and experience many disturbances in our lives. The supreme Being is indivisible light, and we have come like little sparks from that divine light. Due to this separation from our source, the light of supreme Consciousness, we have become entangled in *maya.* The influence of *maya* makes the mind very active, and as we are ruled by the mind, we ruin our lives. We are always restless and disturbed. The mind, influenced by *maya,* is the root cause of all our suffering.

So we need to end the tyranny of the mind. We need to overthrow the sovereignty of the mind—we must not remain under the dominance of the mind. The power of the mind must be completely controlled. That is why the *Khadga Mala* starts with *"Siro Devyai namah:* Salutations to the divine energy that dwells in the brain, the *sahasrara chakra." Siro Devi* is the name given to the brain system, which is the seat of the mind. It is the seat of all our thoughts, all our actions, of everything we do. The mind controls the entire body system. The *tapas* of meditation purifies and subdues the mind and reunites the individual self with the universal Self.

It is very auspicious and beneficial to chant the sacred *Khadga Mala Stotra* in front of the *Sri Chakra*. It is written in the scriptures that there is an ancient and timeless connection between the *Khadga Mala* and the *Sri Chakra*. And when a seeker chants the *Khadga Mala,* it is said that he passes easily through the fifteen *avasthas*. We are all familiar with the states of waking, dreaming, deep sleep and *turiya.* But there are said to be fifteen states, and one who chants the *Khadga Mala Stotra* is able to cross all of them with ease. A seeker must cross these fifteen *avasthas,* states or stages, before he can enter into *maha nirvana*, the sixteenth stage. *Maha nirvana,* the final resting-place, is *moksha*—the complete merging of the individual soul into the supreme Soul. That is why the *Pancha Dashakshari* and *Shodashakshari Mantras* sacred to Devi have fifteen and sixteen *bijaksharas* respectively.

These extremely powerful *mantras* of *Sri Vidya* are not given easily to *sadhakas*. The *Guru* tests the aspirant very strictly and does not initiate anyone into this *mantra* lightly. Only after a very long period of rigorous *sadhana* is a seeker initiated into the *Pancha Dashakshari Mantra,* and much later into the *Shodashakshari Mantra.* When a *Guru* initiates a disciple into any *mantra,* the *shishya* must be educated about the power of that *mantra,* how it should be chanted, as well as when it should be chanted and when it should not. It is the *Guru's* responsibility to teach the disciple all these things. Only those who have dedicated themselves to *Sri Vidya,* that is, those who have vowed to undertake the regular practice of *Sri Vidya upasana,* can be initiated into these *maha mantras* with the blessings of the *Guru*.

When a seeker does *sadhana* following the directions of the *Guru,* gradually crossing the fifteen stages and finally entering the sixteenth stage, the *Maha nirvana avastha* or *moksha,* he never returns to this world—he is never reborn! We pray to Mother Divine with the *shloka* from the *Lalita Sahasranama, "Nirvana sukha dayinyai namo namah:* Salutations again and again to the compassionate Mother who blesses us with *nirvana." "Sukha dayini"* means "Mother Divine is the giver of that eternal joy which is found in the final resting-place."

The *siro sthana,* the *sahasrara,* is the place of eternal *jyoti,* radiant light. It must always be filled with divine effulgence, and radiate its *jyoti* to the entire universe. A devotee of *Sri Vidya,* who practices *Sri Vidya upasana* regularly, becomes an *adhikari,* one entitled to receive initiation into the *Shodashakshari Mantra,* and in time masters *Sri Vidya*. By chanting the *Khadga Mala Stotra* and the sacred *mantras* of *Sri Vidya,* one ultimately attains the *shodasha sthana*.

The *Khadga Mala* bestows us with worldly benefits, too. Suppose we have problems—bad health, lawsuits, or any other difficulties—the *Guru* advises us to chant the *Khadga Mala* in front of the *Sri Chakra*. Many people have experienced that when they did this, they were relieved of the problems and difficulties they had been undergoing. Such is the power of the *Khadga Mala Stotra!* However, such a powerful and secret *stotra* should not be used only for material benefits.

Too many thoughts may disturb us during meditation, or we may have other hindrances in our *sadhana*. If we chant the *Khadga Mala Stotra,* all such problems will be removed, because the *Khadga Mala* is not simply a garland of ordinary names, it is a shining garland of divine light. The *mantras* of the *Khadga Mala* are the subtle, cosmic forms of effulgent divine energies. So when we chant their sacred and powerful names, these energies completely transform our mind, making it still. *Sri Khadga Mala Stotra* helps the *sadhaka* to proceed in *sadhana* very easily and smoothly. Thus we see that the *Khadga Mala Stotra* bestows both worldly and spiritual benefits on seekers.

The *Vedas* are self-born—no one wrote them. They are the manifested form of *Veda Rani, Maha Rani, Sri Vani,* Saraswati Devi, the supreme Goddess of knowledge and wisdom. Mother Divine has blessed us with the greatest boon in the form of the effulgence of the *Vedas,* which are nothing but the embodiment of supreme Consciousness.

Mother has descended in the form of *Sri Vidya* from Her celestial *chintamani griha,* Her magnificent palace of wish-fulfilling precious gems. It is hard to imagine that we could reach the core of that supreme Consciousness! The Divine has come from that unreachable place and touched our hearts. She is drawing us back to Herself. Mother's *chintamani griha* is not a palace of precious gems. It is nothing but *Omkara,* which takes us from the *akara* to the *nirakara*—from our limited individual self to the eternal, formless *Brahman*—that supreme light and energy.

"You are both *akara* and *nirakara*, You are with and without form. You are the *anu,* the atom, and You are also the cosmos! You are *nirguna* as well as *saguna,* attributeless, and also with attributes." We cannot imagine the Supreme in these ways because our minds are limited. If we meditate, if we concentrate on the *bindu,* the symbol of Divine Mother in the innermost triangle of the *Sri Chakra,* our hearts will open. We will see Her divine light within, and also everywhere in the cosmos. We will know that Divinity alone exists!

The holy *rishis* who lived in the time of the *Rig Veda* were enlightened beings. They had light in their minds and light in their hearts, which was reflected in their glowing faces. Whenever anyone came to them, they gave their help with open hearts. We need to be like them. If we meditate, our heart *chakra* will open and we will experience eternal joy. We will be in tune with everyone. So let us all have one heart, one heartbeat, at least for the one or two hours of this program. That is so beautiful!

Now we have *Sri Vidya*. Mother Divine has blessed us with this *Maha Vidya,* this highest education which is beyond imagination.

> *Sarvam shaktimayam:* Everything is Shakti
> *Sarvam devī mayam:* Everything is Divine Mother

There are countless universes in each enclosure of the *Sri Chakra*. The supreme knowledge of *Sri Vidya* has come from the *bindu sthana,* the central point of the *Sri Chakra,* and touched our hearts. Divine Mother has crossed all these enclosures and reached us. Now we have a new life. A new dawn and sunrise has graced us. We have been graced by *Sri Vidya*—by that supreme Consciousness. She has no form but we give Her a form so that we will be able to approach Her as Mother.

I am your mother. Mother is here with you, for you are all meditators. Amma is teaching you about *Sri Vidya* because our minds need to escape their darkness. They are very inconstant, changing from minute to minute, second to second. One moment we are sad, the next, happy; now we are calm, and then angry. Our minds are different throughout the day. This is the ever-changing nature of the mind. But here we are learning that when we worship the *Sri Chakra* and meditate, we will be in bliss forever. We need intense love for *Sri Chakra puja* and firm faith in meditation. If we have a strong thirst to worship the *Sri Chakra,* and meditate regularly, we will attain eternal peace.

We think we have made great progress in the 21st century. But if high technology is so good, then why is there so much destruction in the world today? Why are there so many wars, with so much violence and bloodshed? Scientific discoveries are good, but we have no peace in our lives. We might go to the sun, the moon, the stars, the Milky Way, to all the galaxies, but what is the use of all this if we cause harm to other human beings?

If it were not for Mother Earth, we would not even be here. But do we ever express our gratitude to Mother Earth? No! Instead, we cover the Earth with blood. The Earth should be a place of light, not darkness. Not to condemn the killing of fellow humans is against the *dharma* of every religion in the world. No one should ever kill anyone. Such violence is caused by the negative thoughts in the mind.

The mind is always troubled by negativity, some of which may be caused by the *karmas* of previous births.

The *siro sthana,* the *avyakta sthana,* the thousand petal *sahasrara* lotus, is illumined when we chant the *Khadga Mala*. The *kanti,* radiance, of this powerful *stotra* burns all negativity to ashes. It brings the light of a new dawn into our minds and hearts. This is only possible with the grace of the Divine. Amma expects peace, universal brotherhood. You are on the correct path, children. If you have disturbances in your life caused by previous *karmas,* stay unmoved. Meditate well. Be immovable!

We will soon print the *Khadga Mala Stotra* for you to learn and recite. Some traditional people are unhappy about this. They are good and learned people, but their minds are stuck at one point—like an old record! They feel that the *Khadga Mala* is secret and very sacred. Divine education belongs to everyone, because everyone is divine. I am divine, you are divine, everything in the world is divine because everything is a manifestation of Shakti, supreme energy!

Love this world, children, love nature, but not with a closed mind, not with a closed heart. Become like the holy *rishis* and fill your hearts and minds with the light of divine love, so that your countenance glows with the radiance of that love. If anyone comes to you, be ready to give your help wholeheartedly. It is not easy to achieve this state, but we can become pure when we clean the *hridaya chakra* and the *siro chakra* through spiritual practices.

As these *chakras* are purified, we slowly and gradually go beyond thoughts and desires. We are released from all bondages, and become one with the light of supreme Consciousness. Meditation is the highest *ananda,* for it brings eternal happiness and bliss! It fills us with love of nature, cosmic love, wisdom and all the divine attributes. That is *Sri Vidya*.

ॐ

SRI VIDYA IS OPEN TO ALL

Satyam is Truth. We have spoken about *Satyam*, Truth, in many discourses. *Satyam* is also known by another beautiful and wonderful name, *"Ritambhara prajna*." It is the *turiya* state, the state of *samadhi*, the ultimate state of *yoga*. *Ritambhara prajna* is discussed in *Sri Vidya*.

Sri Vidya also speaks about the different forms of God. Actually many people are confused because there are innumerable Gods and Goddesses with so many different names and forms. Every religion has its own God, but *Sri Vidya* states very clearly that all these forms—for example, Lakshmi Devi, Narasimha Swami, Ganesha, Lord Siva, and countless others—are only different aspects of the one supreme Being,

There are also many different *Gurus*. Each religion or path of spiritual discipline has a different founder. But according to *Sri Vidya*, there is only one God. All the numerous names and forms we use to approach the Divine are illumined by the same divine light, which is one! *Sri Vidya* is very emphatic about this point.

There are many *ashrams*, monasteries and sacred *pithas* or spiritual centers in the world. In each of these, seekers are taught about Truth in different ways. What has happened in the past, and is happening even now, is that these teachings tend to be limited. The teachers stop at certain levels due to their own understanding and beliefs. They cannot go beyond a certain point. And each of them is convinced that his own way of thinking is not only correct, but also the best. This should not happen. Truth is like the holy Ganga, its flow goes on forever. *Sri Vidya* blesses us with the highest knowledge of the Supreme. *Sri Vidya* has existed for countless centuries, for millions and millions of years. Like the holy Ganga, it must flow on forever. But what is happening in the world today is that many restrictions and limitations have been placed upon seekers. The teachers tell them, "You cannot follow this *sadhana* as you are not eligible for it."

This attitude keeps aspirants from worshipping God according to their desire. There are many different ways in which a seeker can approach Divinity, and there should be no restriction at all regarding the path a devotee chooses. The teachings of *Sri Vidya* are very universal. This sacred *vidya* declares that each one of us is eligible to enter the kingdom of the Divine. So everyone should be free to enter the great mansion of *Sri Vidya*; everyone should be inspired to learn *Sri Vidya* and attain the highest destination—eternal liberation!

Many people want to lead a spiritual life, but a spiritual seeker must possess certain qualities. There are three kinds of people in this world. People of the first type are plagued by endless questions and doubts whenever they start something new or undertake any venture. They keep thinking about it, unable to decide whether they should begin it or not. They don't have the balance of mind to make a decision. They are not ready to face or accept whatever comes to them in life.

People belonging to the second category are classed as medium. When they take up some task, if any difficulties or disturbances come up, they cannot tackle these problems. They just give up. Such people are not eligible for spiritual life.

But people of the third type are great! They are very courageous. Whatever task is given to them, or whatever work they themselves choose to undertake, they never hesitate or stop till the goal is reached. They keep working steadily till they achieve success. These are the greatest people in this world. As spiritual aspirants, be like these great persons, not like those of the other two classes.

Sri Vidya is *Maha Vidya*, the highest knowledge. *Sri Vidya* has been compared to a magnificent mansion. But unfortunately, those who have approached this mighty, royal mansion have not been able to enter. Even today, the priests and teachers of this *Maha Sri Vidya* do not allow anyone to enter its gates. They do not permit devotees to chant *Sri Lalita Sahasranama* or any of the *vedic suktas*, or to perform the special *pujas* laid down in *Sri Vidya*. They do not like to share this divine knowledge with anyone. They say that they are the only ones eligible to chant its *mantras*. If anyone begins to repeat these sacred *stotras*, they find fault with you, saying, "You are pronouncing the words the wrong way; you are not chanting the *stotra* correctly." And if a seeker wishes to be initiated into *Sri Vidya*, they ask, "Are you qualified to chant the *Khadga Mala*, or the *vedic suktas*?" If you tell them that you have been chanting *Devi mantras*, they will ask whether you were initiated by a *Guru*. This attitude is very wrong. Even if you have been initiated into *Sri Vidya*, or into a study of the *Vedas*, these teachers do not like it at all.

Sri Vidya is the greatest mansion, but its gates are always closed. Many sacred hymns were composed by women saints, and many of the chapters in the scriptures written by knowledgeable women. Yet the keepers of the gates of the mansion of *Sri Vidya*, the *acharyas* and priests, did not like women to learn *Sri Vidya*. They did not permit them to chant the *stotras* or perform the *pujas* special to *Sri Vidya*. They had very narrow views regarding the eligibility of women.

Now I have come here to open the doors of this mighty palace. The gates are open, children. Let us all enter this grand mansion of *Sri Vidya*, and be drenched in the flood of its supreme light! Just as everyone, no matter who it may be, is very naturally energized and illumined by the rays of the sun, in the same way, everyone who enters the wondrous mansion of *Sri Vidya* will be flooded and drenched by the light of divine knowledge!

At present the world is full of darkness and confusion. Each one of us is searching for peace and light. We can get this *shanti* and *jyoti* from Divinity alone. Not only the few people present here, but everyone in the world is longing for *shanti*. Amma is opening the doors of *Sri Vidya* for the whole world. You need only open your hearts and enter to attain that experience of peace and light

ॐ

SIKHA DEVI BESTOWS COMPLETE INWARDNESS

Śrī vidyām jagatām dhātrīm sṛṣṭi sthiti layeśvarīm
Namāmi lalitām nityām mahā tripura sundarīm

Yā devī sarva bhūteṣu śakti rūpeṇa samsthitā
Namastasyai namastasyai namastasyai namo namaḥ

Om hrīmkārāsana garbhitānala śikhām
Sauḥ klīm kalām bibhratīm
Sauvaṇāmbara dhāriṇīm vara sudhām
Dhautām trinetrojjvalām
Vande pustaka pāśamānkuśa dharām
Srag bhūṣitām ujjvalām
Tvām gaurīm tripurām parātpara kalām
Śrī cakra sancāriṇīm

Embodiments of Divine Souls, Amma's Most Beloved Children,

I love you so much!

Sikha Devi is the presiding deity of the third *chakra* mentioned in the *Khadga Mala*. It is a very powerful *chakra,* and has a direct connection to the *sahasrara chakra* as well as the *ajna chakra*. During meditation it receives strong impulses from both these *chakras*.

When you meditate, you must sit straight up, keeping the spine upright. The neck must be aligned with the spine. The head, too, should not bend forward—it should be held straight up. When a *sadhaka* sits in this posture for meditation, there is a tremendous concentration of spiritual energy at the *ajna chakra*—the place of the third eye between the eyebrows—during the peak of meditation. This is the time when the seeker enters the *turiya* state, the thought-free state of *samadhi.* As the *sadhaka* continues to meditate regularly, he may reach this peak state after half an hour or several hours of meditation. In time, every dedicated seeker attains the blissful state of *samadhi.*

So what happens at that time? The divine spiritual energy, highly concentrated at the *ajna chakra* during the peak of meditation, travels to the back of the head where *Sikha Devi* resides in the *sikha chakra.* Located in the medulla oblongata at the back of the brain, this is a very important and wonderful place in our brain system. The *sushumna nadi* and all the *chakras* are energized from this center. We touch it when we perform *anga nyasa* during *pujas.*

We all know about the seven *chakras,* but actually there are innumerable *chakras* in our body. And all these *chakras* are stimulated during meditation in one way or another. When we are in the *turiya* state, completely absorbed in meditation, a brilliant ray of divine light flashes like lightning into the atmosphere from the *sikha sthana,* the *sikha chakra.* It blazes into outer space, penetrates the atmosphere, and reaches the realm of supreme light, supreme Consciousness! This happens only in the peak stage of meditation, the *samadhi* state.

We need to understand the importance of meditation and experience the *turiya* state. People who have been completely purified by meditation carry a very special energy around them. We are attracted to them because the radiant light of divine energy surrounds them all the time. Such noble souls have the ability to perform extraordinary and unbelievable things because of this special energy in their bodies. There is so much energy in them that they can accomplish anything!

We are ordinary human beings, unable to handle or complete even small tasks. But through regular meditation we can get immense energy and do wonderful things in this world—that is how all the noble souls get the energy to perform incredible deeds. People who do not understand the meaning and value of meditation sometimes criticize those who practice it, saying, "You are closing your eyes and escaping from the world, just sitting in one place doing nothing." Those who have not experienced meditation speak in this way, but here the doors of meditation are open, and if you meditate regularly, you can experience the truth about meditation for yourselves.

So, children, the *Sikha Devi chakra,* the third *mantra* in the *Khadga Mala,* is a very powerful subtle center. It is connected to the *sahasrara* as well as the *ajna chakra.* It is a very important *chakra* in the human body. During meditation, it receives strong impulses from the *ajna chakra.* Due to its direct connection with the *ajna chakra,* the meditative energy in the *Sikha Devi chakra* leads the subtle body of the *sadhaka* into the atmosphere. In the form of a strong beam of divine light it pierces through the atmosphere and reaches the luminous stream of supreme Consciousness! So when this *chakra* gets stimulated through regular *dhyana,* it sends strong vibrations of spiritual energy into our subtle body, energizing the whole *sushumna nadi.*[16]

There are innumerable *chakras* in our body. When we meditate intensely for long periods of time, all these *chakras* get stimulated and opened. And at last we reach that final resting place, the *janma, mrityu, jara vishranti*

---

[16] *sushumnā nāḍī:* (*nadi:* tube, vessel, vein) According to *Raja yoga,* the *nadis* are subtle nerve channels through which *prana*, vital energy, flows to all parts of the body. *Nadis* are associated with the subtle body, and though they may have some correspondence with their physical counterparts, cannot actually be seen. There are 72,000 *nadis*, the most important being the *sushumna*. The *ida* or *chandra* (moon) *nadi* lies to the left of the *sushumna*, and the *pingala* or *surya* (sun) *nadi* lies to its right.

sthana, that place of complete peace beyond birth, old age and death, reaching which we never return to this world.

As the *Sikha Devi chakra* gets stimulated, it begins to open, together with many other very powerful *chakras.* When this happens, the *sadhaka* attains unbelievable memory power and concentration. He is infused with self-confidence and very naturally develops right thinking. He can easily accomplish any work in this world—any task that is assigned to him, or that he has chosen for himself. Such people succeed in whatever they do.

This *Sikha Devi chakra* not only makes us healthy, giving us a strong body and mind, it also blesses us with great spiritual strength. When this *chakra* is enhanced, that is, when it is completely purified and begins to glow once more with its natural effulgence, it also strengthens the *sushumna nadi*. The *sushumna nadi* is a subtle nerve which runs through the spine, connecting the *muladhara chakra* to the *sahasrara*—the root *chakra* to the crown *chakra*. And during meditation, as the *Sikha Devi chakra* energizes the *sushumna nadi,* the *kundalini,* the divine spiritual energy, awakens and begins to rise upward from the *muladhara chakra.* The *Sikha Devi chakra* helps the sleeping *kundalini* to awaken. And when it is awakened, it passes through all the *shad chakras,* the six *chakras* in the *sushumna nadi,* finally reaching the *sahasrara*. So we see that the *Sikha Devi chakra* plays a very important role in *kundalini* awakening.

You all know that the *muladhara chakra* is the root *chakra* at the base of the spine. The *kundalini* lies asleep in the *muladhara.* It is only through *yoga* and the regular practice of meditation that the *kundalini* can be activated and awakened. Because of the *samskaras* and *karma* load of countless previous births, it is very difficult to awaken the dormant *kundalini.* But when we begin to perform our spiritual practices seriously, with intensity and earnestness, all the mountains of *karmas* are burned in the *muladhara chakra* itself. Only then does the *kundalini* awaken and begin its upward journey through the *sushumna nadi* to the *sahasrara*.

Sri Vidya has spoken very extensively about *kundalini shakti.* You may have heard about *kundalini,* or read about it in various books. These days many books dealing with the *chakras* and *kundalini* are available. But the explanations in these books differ from author to author, so that the true concept of the *chakras* and even the diagrams are completely changed. The original flavor is altogether lost. The information in these books is incorrect. Only *Sri Vidya* has gone deeply into the subject of *kundalini,* and only this *Maha Vidya* discusses in detail how the divine energy *kundalini* can be awakened through the *yoga* of meditation.

Our *muladhara* is completely blocked by the *samskaras* we bring with us from innumerable previous lives. So this root *chakra* must be thoroughly purified before the *kundalini* can awaken. All the *samskaras* in the *muladhara chakra* need to be completely burned in *dhyana agni,* the blazing fire of meditative energy—not the slightest trace of any active *samskaras* must be left. Only then will the spiritual energy, *kundalini,* awaken and rise from the *muladhara* to the *next chakra,* the *svadhishthana.*

And what will our nature be when we become such a *sadhaka?* We will not give any importance to the body; our mind will always be turned inward. We will have no interest in the world—we will be completely detached from worldly matters. We see some rare individuals like this around us. But until every single *samskara* has been burned to ashes by our regular practice of meditation, we will remain stuck at the *muladhara*—the *kundalini shakti* will not awaken and move upward.

In one of the *mantras* of *Sri Lalita Sahasranama,* Mother has been praised as *"Pancha pretasanasina:* Sri Lalita Devi is seated on a throne formed by the five lifeless deities." Actually, this name does not merely praise Mother Divine, it speaks of the greatest *yoga*. What does this *mantra* really mean according to *Sri Vidya?* Mother's seat is in the *sahasrara,* the crown *chakra.* But all the *shad chakras,* our other six *chakras,* are at different stages, where countless *samskaras* are accumulated. All of these—each and every one of them—must be burned. The layers of impurities have to be removed and all the knots in the *chakras* released. The activity of all the *samskaras* at each center must be completely silenced and stilled. Due to certain deeply-rooted desires, *samskaras,* which are still active in the *chakras,* we get stuck at some points; we get blocked there. When every *chakra* becomes a cremation ground, and every single desire is reduced to ashes like a burnt corpse, then only will Mother, the supreme Consciousness, be permanently established on Her royal throne in the *sahasrara chakra*.

The second *chakra,* the *svadhishthana,* is controlled by the *Sikha Devi chakra,* which is situated in the medulla oblongata at the back of the head. The *svadhishthana* is another important *chakra* for the spiritual aspirant. All the good and bad desires reside here, blocking one's spiritual progress. This *chakra* is strictly and very well controlled by the *Sikha Devi chakra.* Sometimes we commit mistakes unknowingly—we almost seem to be forced into doing things we know we should not do. It is our *samskaras* that make us act in this way. But there is an inner voice which always instructs and guides us—it warns us when we are tempted to do something wrong. When we are confused, the inner voice tells us, "It is not right to act in this way." We often get this kind of guidance. From where does this inner intuition come? It comes from the S*ikha Devi chakra*.

In very difficult situations we also get guidance from the *sahasrara.* But sometimes we do not listen to these warnings, and keep making the same mistakes again and again. This happens when our *samskaras* are very strong.

The first three *chakras* are very important. Once we cross them, our further progress becomes easier. But it is very difficult to cross the *muladhara* and *svadhishthana chakras.* That is why we need to remain in silence and do a great deal of meditation.

There are numerous books, pictures and journals about *kundalini vidya,* but in all of these, so many things about *kundalini* have been distorted. Actually, *kundalini vidya,* the true knowledge of *kundalini shakti,* is hidden in *Sri Vidya* in the *Lalita Sahasranama Stotra.* Innumerable secrets about the divine energy *kundalini* are embedded in the *mantras* of *Sri Lalita Sahasranama. Pancha pretasanasina* is one such *mantra.* Other beautiful *mantras* are *Bhavani, Bhavana gamya, Bhavaranya kutharika*[17]—*kutharika* is a sword and *bhava* means our *samaskaras. Bhavaranya* is a dense forest full of huge trees. This dense forest indicates our *karma* load.

When we lead a spiritual life and meditate on the original source of all energy—Mother, in the form of the divine energy *kundalini* in the *muladhara*—this root *chakra* opens. Then the *bhavaranya,* the dense forest of our *samskaras,* is immediately burned by the fire of meditation. This fire is not an ordinary fire. It is *yoga agni, jnana agni, Siva agni*—the fire of *yoga,* the fire of true knowledge, the fire of Lord Siva Himself! Everything is burned to ashes by the power of this divine energy. *Yoga agni* is the sword—*kutharika*—that immediately cuts all the *samskaras* in the root *chakra.*

---

[17] *Lalitā Sahasranāma,* names 112-114.

All the *chakras* are connected to one another. The *muladhara* is connected to the *svadhishthana,* the *svadhishthana* to the *manipura*, the *manipura* to the *anahata* or heart *chakra,* the heart *chakra* to the *ajna chakra,* and the *ajna chakra* to the *sahasrara.* But these are not the only *chakras* in our body. We have thousands of small *chakras* and sub-*chakras* in the body, with countless connections to each other!

We feel our physical body, and we are aware of our mental body. We are always entangled in our thoughts. Sometimes we suffer because we are sad or angry, and there are times when we are full of negative thoughts and feelings. But you are not the physical, mental or intellectual bodies, you are the supreme Self! But because you believe you are the body, you never think, "This physical body does not belong to me. Neither do the mental and intellectual bodies belong to me. My real body is only divine light!"

If you believe you are the subtle body of light, you can easily go anywhere. In a fraction of a second you can travel to India, Germany, Australia, or to any part of the cosmos, *anywhere!* The subtle body can even go through a wall! You can travel with ease through the universe and come back to this world in seconds! But you need to believe in the subtle body.

Therefore *Sri Vidya* does not discuss the physical, mental or intellectual bodies; it speaks only of the subtle body, our real body. The *kundalini yoga* in *Maha Vidya* and *Sri Lalita Sahasranama* is very, very beautiful. It talks only about the divine light. We need that kind of strong and correct knowledge about *kundalini shakti.* And then, once we start practicing this *yoga vidya,* all the *karma* load accumulated in the *muladhara* through millions of lives, all of the *bhavaranya,* is totally burned by the power of meditation. The *kundalini* immediately awakens in the root *chakra* and begins to move upward towards the next *chakra,* the *svadhishthana.*

All the *mantras* about the *kundalini,* the *muladhara* and *svadhishthana chakras* in the *Lalita Sahasranama* are closely connected with the *Sri Chakra*. We have a beautiful *Sri Chakra* in our bodies, children, and according to *Sri Vidya,* there are thousands of enchanting colors in our natural body, the body of light. Mother in the *sahasrara* is extolled as "*Sarva varnopa shobhita*:[18] She glows with all the colors!" So we are not just bones, blood or nerves, we are not just hearts and pulses—we are the supreme light! *Sri Vidya* specifically discusses our supreme Self. And where is that supreme Self? It resides in the form of the divine *kundalini shakti* in the root *chakra*.

There are five *vayus* or *pranas,* five kinds of vital breath, in our body: *prana, apana, vyana, udana* and *samana*. When we expand these vital energies, all the *chakras*—such as the *Siro Devi, Sikha Devi, Astra Devi* and the heart *chakra*—are stimulated, and the *kundalini* immediately travels through them all and reaches the *sahasrara*. I have not found this secret in any of the modern books. Instead, these books might have beautiful color plates, but these pictures vary according to the understanding and vision of the writer. We can find some original diagrams of the *kundalini* in ancient texts, but in modern art the colors are often modified. We cannot change the colors of the *chakras*. Each *chakra* has its own natural color.

The *muladhara chakra* is a beautiful four petal lotus where Lord Ganesha resides. Sri Ganesha is nothing but *Adi Para Shakti,* and *Adi Para Shakti* is nothing but the *Nirakara Para Brahma,* the formless, supreme *Brahman,* the Absolute. We call this supreme Divinity by many

---

[18] *Lalitā Sahasranāma,* name 529.

names, such as Ganesha, Lakshmi, Lalitambika, Mother Divine, and so on. But *Adi Para Shakti,* the supreme Energy, is one—only one! So *kundalini vidya* speaks only about light, not names or forms. *Adi Para Shakti* can manifest in any form dear to the heart of the devotee. But it is formless, it is divine radiance, it is oneness, oneness, oneness!

When we always begin our meditation with *pranayama,* over time, after many long sittings, the *yoga agni* of *dhyana* gradually makes the root *chakra* shine with stainless purity. All the *samskaras* in the *muladhara* are burned and the bonds of *maya* released. We experience our body as separate from our Self. We see very clearly: "This body does not belong to me—I am not the body!"

When you reach this stage, it makes no difference whether anyone praises you or calls you names. You always remain calm and unmoved—you have become a *sthita prajna,* one firmly established in wisdom. You remain polite and friendly towards everyone because you know that you are not the body. Your permanent name is "the Self." You have no other name, so how can you respond to any name? We react to praise and blame because we are in body-consciousness. When we meditate deeply, we go beyond body-consciousness, and then the *kundalini shakti* begins to move upward towards the second *chakra,* the *svadhishthana.*

As we continue our *sadhana* of meditation, gradually all the *chakras* are cleaned and begin to glow. We go into deep states of *dhyana* when we close our eyes and turn inward. Then the divine *kundalini* energy travels joyfully and playfully upward, against the natural law of gravity. In this world, if anything happens to an airplane, it just comes down and lands somewhere—maybe in a river or in the sea. The only energy in the world that naturally travels upward through the *chakras* and reaches the highest Consciousness, cosmic Consciousness, is the *kundalini shakti*. Everything in this world is attracted to the Earth; only the awakened *kundalini* travels upward towards the head, taking the *sadhaka* to higher levels of consciousness.

India, or Bharata, is not a country; it is not a land, it is a *samskriti,* a divine culture. This land is simply divine culture. In ancient times, the holy *rishis* meditated in this sacred land called *Bharatavarsha.* They practiced *yoga,* they meditated on *kundalini,* and they experienced the divine light, the cosmic light, within themselves. They also saw the same cosmic energy in the trees and birds and flowers—everywhere in the whole universe!

Whenever these holy ones picked a flower from a plant, they first prayed to Mother Earth, "Mother, Mother, Mother! My Mother, my beloved Mother, please forgive me. Forgive me, O Mother!" They spoke to Mother Earth as their very own mother. "Mother, please forgive me, I want to pluck this beautiful flower. The blossom is not for any person, it is for *puja,* the worship of the Divine. So Mother, please forgive me."

When they wanted to cut down a tree, they asked for forgiveness. And when they wanted to collect the sap from a tree by making a cut in its trunk, they also prayed for forgiveness. If they cut down one tree, they planted a thousand cuttings from its branches to grow a thousand new trees. They wanted to protect Mother Nature—the trees, plants, flowers and water. Nobody thought of Bharata as land. They thought of her as their mother. And the Motherland belonged to everybody in the world.

Because these wise, noble and saintly people sat on the earth of this land and meditated, they not only made it sacred, they brought peace to the entire world. They expected and prayed for peace for everyone in the whole world. They expected peace, but we do not expect peace, and we do not have peace in our lives. We are immersed in worldly intoxication; we are absorbed in our own selfish interests; we never think about others.

The holy *rishis* thought about everyone. They were established in divine light, they were *themselves* light, and that is why they expected that light for everyone. We need to experience that divine light. We need to love this world and bless this world. So, my dear children, fill your hearts with the divine light of devotion and love, and share that light with the entire world!

Om asato mā sad gamaya
Tamaso mā jyotir gamaya
Mṛtyor mā amṛtam gamaya

Om śānti śanti śantiḥ

Lokāḥ samastāḥ sukhino bhavantu 3x

ॐ

BLESSINGS OF SIKHA DEVI AND NETRA DEVI

Śrī vidyām jagatām dhātrīm sṛṣṭi sthiti layeśvarī
Namāmi lalitām nityām mahā tripura sundarī

Yā devī sarva bhūteṣu śakti rūpeṇa samsthitā
Namastasyai namastasyai namastasyai namo namaḥ

Children,

The *Sikha Devi chakra* has a very special *yogic shakti*, or *yogic* energy, known as *unmani. Unmani* is such a beautiful word! In *Sri Lalita Sahasranama,* Divine Mother has been praised in one of the *mantras* as *Manonmani.*[19] *"Mana"* means "the mind," and "*unmani"* means "withdrawn mind." Mother creates the world, but She is detached from it. She is the one who transforms our mind by calming it and turning it inward. Every spiritual aspirant strives earnestly and works hard to become inward, but inwardness is not easy to attain. The *Sikha Devi chakra* bestows its own *yogic* energy, *unmani,* the rare quality of complete detachment, on the *sadhaka,* making it easy for him to turn his mind inward and break the bonds of worldly attachment.

There are four important points to remember about the *Sikha Devi chakra.* As you know, the divine spiritual energy, *kundalini,* lies asleep in the *muladhara chakra.* Before we begin our *sadhana* for *kundalini*-awakening, the mind must be completely silenced and turned inward. The first important quality that the *Sikha Devi chakra* bestows on us is complete and absolute inwardness.

The second blessing we get from this powerful *chakra* is the experience of *videha sthiti,* the bodiless state. *Videha sthiti* is the state in which, even though we are in the body,

[19] *Lalitā Sahasranāma,* name 207.

we are completely detached from it. We don't give any importance to the body—we don't think about it at all.

The third important function of the *Sikha Devi chakra* is that it brightens the *anahata chakra,* the heart *chakra,* situated in the *dahara akasha,* the inner sky of the heart, the inner Self. When the *dahara akasha* is filled with divine radiance, the heart of the *sadhaka* becomes very soft and compassionate, and he develops universal love and understanding.

The fourth and most important action of this divine *Sikha Devi chakra* is it helps the *kundalini* to ascend from *chakra* to *chakra*. There are many interconnections between the innumerable *chakras* in our body, and many hidden *yogic* secrets in *Sri Vidya*. Powerful *bijakshara mantras* are given to *Sri Vidya* practitioners so that they can enhance the *chakras* by concentrating on the sacred seed letters. The powerful vibrations of these *bijaksharas* purify *sadhakas* at all levels, so that they are able to progress quickly in their *sadhana*.

When the *kundalini* reaches the *ajna chakra* with the help of the *Sikha Devi chakra,* the aspirant is completely absorbed in deep meditation and sees everything as universal light! All illusion disappears and the mind becomes completely still and silent. This state is extremely difficult to reach, but the *sadhaka* can attain it with divine grace. But sometimes the spiritual energy gets blocked in certain *chakras,* and we have to struggle very hard to transcend those places. Only through the *yoga* of regular meditation, combined with the blessing of divine grace, can that high state be achieved.

And what happens when the *sadhaka* reaches that beautiful place? He feels that the whole world is saturated with the pure light of the *Atman,* with the divine effulgence of God, the Almighty! He sees everything as divine Consciousness alone.

This is a very wonderful feeling, but we have to go even beyond this stage. In order to attain the ultimate goal of spiritual *sadhana,* we need to be permanently established in the *sahasrara,* the crown *chakra*. It is only in the *sahasrara* that we get the realization, "I am the *Atman,* I am God! My Self is the divine light that is supreme Consciousness! I am Divinity, I am the supreme Being!" This ultimate and supremely blissful state of Self-Realization is not attained in the *ajna chakra;* it is experienced in the *sahasrara* alone.

Netra Devi Mantra: The next *mantra* in the *Khadga Mala* is *Kavacha Devi,* which we will discuss later. Skipping ahead to the *mantra Netra Devyai namah,* the *Netra Devi chakra* is located between the two *netras,* the eyes. You know it as the *ajna chakra.* In *Sri Vidya,* the *ajna chakra* is called *Netra Devi*. What happens to the *sadhaka* when the spiritual energy, *kundalini,* reaches the *ajna chakra?* He is not in this world. He has no external vision at all. Even though his eyes are open, he sees nothing! Such is the power of the *Netra Devi chakra* that when the *kundalini* is established in it, the world becomes invisible to the aspirant.

In *Sri Vidya, bijaksharas* are very important. The *Saraswati Mantra* contains *Om* and three prime seed letters, *Aim, Srim* and *Hrim*. The *mantras* of *Sri Vidya,* too, have the same *bijaksharas,* but they are in a different order—*Om, Aim, Hrim, Srim*. All *Devi Mantras* in *Sri Vidya* start with these *bijaksharas.*

Bhaskarananda Swami was a very staunch follower of *Sri Vidya.* During a brief period, he was responsible for spreading the knowledge of this great *Maha Vidya* in India. He was from Andhra Pradesh, and he traveled to Karnataka State, teaching *Sri Vidya* to some deserving devotees. In those days only a few seekers were interested in this *Atma Vidya*. Bhaskarananda Swami taught the devotees how to chant the *Khadga Mala* and other *Devi Stotras,* such as *Sri Lalita Sahasranama.*

In *Sri Vidya,* the most important seed letter is *Srim*. Children, you repeat this sacred *bijakshara* innumerable times daily when you chant the *Saraswati Mantra,* the *Sri Suktam,* the *Samputita Sri Suktam,* the *Lakshmi Devi Mantra* or other *vedic shlokas*. So in a way, without knowing it, you have already been practicing *Sri Vidya upasana!* You are all really very fortunate and blessed— you have been worshipping Divine Mother by chanting the *Srim bijakshara* so many times in the *Sri Suktam,* the *Lalita Sahasranama* and many other *stotras* and *mantras* sacred to Devi.

And you are very fortunate if you have the *Sri Chakra* in your home. Even if you don't know anything about the *Sri Chakra,* just having it in any form is enough—it brings you the blessings of *Sri Vidya.* Even a small *Sri Chakra* attracts billions of cosmic rays and transmits them to the *chakras* in our body. So it is very beneficial and auspicious to sit reverently in front of the *Sri Chakra* and chant the *Sri Suktam, Sri Lalita Sahasranama,* or some other *mantras.*

Swamiji: We are indeed very fortunate and blessed that Mother Herself has come in this form to teach us, and has been inspiring us to practice *Sri Vidya upasana,* though we have not even been aware of it!

[Amma laughs]

Amma: The *Netra Devi chakra* has great *yogic* importance, and it is the place on which *sadhakas* generally concentrate when they meditate. During the peak time of *dhyana,* aspirants can feel strong vibrations as the spiritual energy gets highly concentrated at the *ajna chakra.* They also experience light. And three things happen when the *kundalini* gets stabilized at the *Netra Devi chakra:*

The *sadhaka* achieves *drishya shunyata.* This is a very beautiful term! In this state, even with the eyes open, nothing is seen! Let me explain: Our eyes are merely instruments. When we look at a flower, they simply convey the image to the mind. It is the mind which interprets the image, and then we know that we are looking at a flower. The same process applies to every object we perceive.

So what happens when the divine energy reaches the *Netra Devi chakra?* How do we achieve *drishya shunyata,* in which every object disappears? The mind is in complete silence, and does not respond to the images sent by the eyes. That is why, even though our eyes are open, we cannot see anything. Our vision is on a different plane—it is totally inward.

The second thing the *sadhaka* achieves is *bhava shunyata,* in which there is no trace of either feelings or imagination. Sometimes people begin to imagine things while they meditate, and this deviates their mind from the object of meditation—divine Consciousness. They may get agitated or restless. But when the *kundalini* reaches the *Netra Devi chakra,* neither emotion nor imagination can disturb the *sadhaka.*

The third thing the aspirant achieves very naturally is *vastu shunyata,* that is, all objects vanish due to *drishya shunyata.* The silenced mind is incapable of relating to any object.

So, in that elevated *yogic* state the *sadhaka* has no external vision, sees no object, and is not influenced either by feelings or imagination. This is how *Sri Vidya* describes the state of the seeker in whom the divine energy has stabilized at the *Netra Devi* chakra.

Drishya shunyata is also described as *purnima drishti,* or *turiya drishti.* What is *purnima drishti? "Purnima"* means "full moon," and *"drishti"* means "sight." It is the ultimate vision. It is known as *turiya drishti* because it is the *yogic* vision of supreme Consciousness, attained in the fourth state—beyond waking, dreaming and deep sleep—the luminous and eternally blissful state of *samadhi.*

Let me explain *purnima drishti* more clearly: Sometimes, when we go to a temple or are in the presence of a *mahatma,* a holy person, we get into an unusual spiritual state. In that state, even as we are looking at the image of the temple deity or at the *mahatma,* their form disappears! And in its place we see only a mass of light, just brilliant, radiant light! Sometimes it becomes dark, and we cannot see anything at all. We get such experiences when we attain a certain level in our meditation—when the divine energy, *kundalini,* reaches and enters the *sahasrara chakra.* That is when such visions are seen.

We are under the influence of many impurities, the inner enemies in the form of vices such as desire, anger, greed, pride, jealousy and hatred. So what happens when we are on the *yogic* path and start meditating regularly? All these inner enemies, all these vices, are transformed by the *yogic* energy of meditation into divine attributes. All our negativity slowly and gradually subsides. It leaves our heart. We are completely transformed by the power of *yogic* energy; every pore of our being is drenched with divine energy. This *divya shakti* increases with the progress of our regular *sadhana* and, in time, we are blessed with *purnima drishti.* Then we do not see any object, we see only divine light!

The *Sri Vidya* tradition also speaks about *srishti,* creation. We have many questions and doubts about the creation of this universe. *Sri Vidya* explains beautifully, in a very clear and methodical way, how the universe came into existence. The whole universe is a manifestation of *akhanda Chaitanya,* indivisible divine Consciousness.

Before the universe came into being, there was only the light of *akhanda Chaitanya.* And from that supreme Consciousness was born *kala,* time itself. And then from *kala,* there emerged a triangle-shaped energy. The three angles of this triangle consisted of the three prime seed letters, *Aim, Hrim* and *Srim.* All the universes were born from a spark of the energy of this triangle.

In *Sri Vidya,* in the *Lalita Sahasranama Stotra* and *Khadga Mala,* there are some *mantras* in which Divine Mother has been praised as *Kalpantara sthayini.* What does this beautiful name mean? "That which is beyond imagination!" *Kalpantara sthayini* is the name of that eternal energy which was ever there—before the creation of all the universes. The creation and destruction of the cosmos has taken place countless times. That supreme energy, or supreme Consciousness, is the sole witness of all the cycles of creation and dissolution.

When *kundalini* reaches the *Netra Devi chakra,* the secret of creation is revealed to the seeker. In no other writings, in no other literature in the world, can we find the description of the creation of the universe as explained in *Sri Vidya*.

The ancient sages meditated and practiced intense *tapas.* The holy *rishis* were seers, who saw the Truth. They spoke about creation after they had themselves seen it in meditation. Not even Brahma, the Creator Himself, Vishnu or Maheshwara know the inner secrets of this creation!

We can get an idea about this by studying the diagram of the *Sri Chakra*. It shows us all the different triangles. First, look at the center point, which is a small circle or dot. This central spot is called the *bindu*. This *bindu sthana,* the place of the *bindu,* is indivisible Consciousness, known as *akhanda Chaitanya.* And when you look at the *bindu,* immediately around it you will see an inverted triangle. The triangle does not point upward, it points downward. Every triangle has three angles, as we know. And the angles of this divine inverted triangle are the three sacred *bijaksharas, Aim, Hrim* and *Srim*.

So from that triangle emerged all the universes we see in the cosmos—all the planets, all the stars and galaxies! Not just one universe, innumerable universes were born. And the one Truth which embodies all these universes is called *Brahmanda bhandodari*—Divine Mother has been praised as *Brahmanda bhandodari* because She is the one who contains all the universes in creation within Her womb.

Nanna, do you know the *Brahmanda bhandodari* song? It is so beautiful! I would like to show you a picture of that *Brahmanda bhandodari.* In the cosmos, Divine Mother takes thousands of forms. Actually, Mother is formless. But She is divine energy, and that energy divides itself into two parts—Siva and Shakti. So the first form of Divine Mother is Siva. Actually, as I just said, Mother is formless *Brahman,* the Absolute. But the formless *Brahman* divided into the forms of Siva and Shakti. Innumerable forms came from that supreme *Shakti*—innumerable *brahmandas* or universes, with their suns, moons and planets. Millions of stars, the Milky Way, and countless galaxies appeared. These issued in a continuous and spontaneous stream from the center point, the *bindu* in the innermost triangle of the *Sri Chakra.*

The *bindu* is nothing but *Pranava* or *Omkara;* it is divine light! And from that light emerged the inverted triangle with the prime *bijaksharas, Aim, Hrim* and *Srim*. The triangle is not just an ordinary drawing. It depicts the supreme energy which manifested in that form. And gradually the whole universe emerged from that energy triangle.

This universe began to expand and multiply, giving birth to many other universes. As this was happening, a bright beam of light flooded forth from the *bindu sthana* in the form of a straight line, dividing the cosmos into two. It kept changing direction, dividing and re-dividing the cosmos. That is how we got the eight directions.

After the directions, the next to be born from that *akhanda Chaitanya* were the *pancha bhutas,* the five basic elements of nature. Earth, being a planet as well as one of the five *pancha bhutas*, was already present in the universe. But until the creation of the *pancha bhutas,* there was no life on Earth. With the creation of water, life appeared on Earth. Water is the main source of life for plants and trees. With the formation of oceans and rivers, first came plant life, then insects, birds, reptiles, mammals and other animals, and finally human beings appeared. It is stated in *Sri Vidya* that 8,400,000 species were created at that time! This is how creation is described in *Sri Vidya.*

The *bindu* is the center point of the *Sri Chakra,* and is the very source of universal energy. It is the source of the entire cosmos. As the *bindu* is the starting point of everything, mathematically we can call it "number one." And then comes the triangle which emerges from that *bindu.* Supreme Consciousness manifests in the form of a luminous triangle which consists of the three sacred *bijaksharas: Aim, Hrim* and *Srim.* 1 + 3 = 4.

A beautiful *mantra* in *Sri Lalita Sahasranama* praises Divine Mother as *Chatur bahu samanvita.*[20] The literal meaning of this Sanskrit name is that Divine Mother has four arms. *"Chatur"* means "four," but its spiritual or *yogic* meaning is *"ananta." "Ananta"* means "infinite," that is, innumerable, beyond imagination.

The four arms of Devi represent the four *bijaksharas: Om, Aim, Hrim* and *Srim. Chatur* also depicts the countless forms of Mother. Therefore it is clear that no one created the universe. The cosmic light of supreme Consciousness itself began to expand and became the entire universe. This is how the process of creation has been explained in *Sri Vidya*. The *bindu* expanded itself into the universe, and this universe is still expanding!

There is no difference between supreme Consciousness and the *trikona,* for the triangle is simply a manifestation of *Chaitanya*. But, as soon as it emerges from that one Consciousness, we see it as different—we don't see it as one with *Chaitanya*. We say that the *bindu* came first and the triangle appeared after it. So, the moment the triangle manifests, *maya* appears! We begin to see difference in

---

[20] *Lalitā Sahasranāma,* name 7.

unity; we experience duality. People may ask, "Why is *maya* created? Why does Mother Herself cast *maya* on us?" [Laughter] *Maya* and creation are born together!

Let me explain more clearly: The *Aim, Hrim* and *Srim bijaksharas* of the triangle are the subtle forms of the three prime *shaktis,* energies—Maha Lakshmi, Maha Saraswati and Maha Kali. The moment they appear, these three divine forms give rise to dualistic thinking, for we see them as different from one another, as well as different from supreme Consciousness. That is how *Maha Maya* is automatically created! And that is why, in *Sri Vidya,* Divine Mother Herself is extolled as *Maha Maya.*[21]

Sri Vidya has approached us to remove the veil of *maya*. The highest knowledge, the greatest education of *Sri Vidya* has come to us to lift us from duality into oneness. The powerful *Khadga Mala mantras* bestow true knowledge upon us and cause us to lose our separate individual identity. As we repeat the sacred Devi names in the *Khadga Mala,* we begin to realize that we are an indivisible part of the Divine, even though we appear to be separate from it. We experience that we are one with the divine light of Consciousness.

When we meditate on the energies in the *Khadga Mala,* they raise us to higher levels of spirituality and merge us with the *bindu sthana,* the eternal abode of supreme Consciousness. The *bindu sthana* is the *mula sthana,* the source of universal energy, also known as *Amba. "Amba"* means Mother, Amma. So that is how Divine Mother came to be—when we gave form to that Consciousness.

The *Prashna Upanishad* is well known. *"Prashna"* means question. In this beautiful *Upanishad,* sincere seekers ask innumerable questions, to which answers are given. All the *Upanishads* were born from *Sri Vidya,* so they have a close connection to this *Maha Vidya*. The

[21] *Lalitā Sahasranāma,* name 215.

knowledge of *Sri Vidya* is to be found in a simplified form in the *Upanishads.* In the *Prashna Upanishad* there is a very beautiful *shloka* which begins with the words:

> *Om pūrṇamadaḥ pūrṇamidam*
>
> Everything we find in the universe is complete. Nothing is incomplete.

The *bindu* is a central point, a very small dot or circle which is always complete. It can never be incomplete, like a line. And from that *purna,* completeness, emerged the triangle which expanded to manifest all the universes. That is why the *bindu sthana* is called Mother, for all creation was born from it. Everything we see in this world—all the countless forms and names—is nothing but the effulgent manifestation of Divine Mother Herself.

So this *shloka* in the *Prashna Upanishad* praises Divinity with the words:

> *Om pūrṇamadaḥ pūrṇamidam pūrṇāt*
> *Pūrṇam udacyate pūrṇasya pūrṇamādāya*
> *Pūrṇam evā vaśiṣyate*
>
> Your creation is complete. You are complete. You are the source of creation, which is also complete. Nothing is incomplete

No questions at all. We argue about things and say, "Why is the world like this? It should not be this way, it should be different."

Creation is whole and complete. But the nature of divine Consciousness is expansion, so there is no end to this creation—it is ever expanding! It goes on forever and ever. And when the time comes for it to dissolve, Mother absorbs it back into Herself, for She is *Tirodhana kari*[22]—the one who merges it back into its source.

Devi is also praised as *Trikona janani,* the Mother who gave birth to the prime triangle. "How can Mother come in the shape of a triangle?" one may ask. It is not an ordinary triangle. From the *bindu sthana,* the universal source of energy, the divine *shaktis,* energies, Maha Lakshmi, Maha Saraswati and Maha Kali manifested in the form of a divine, radiant triangle! That is why Mother is called *Trikona janani*.

There are countless *stotras* and *shlokas* describing Mother's infinite names and forms. All the hidden secrets of *Sri Vidya* are preserved in the *Khadga Mala Stotra*. When we open the book, chant the divine names and then meditate on them, all the secrets embedded in the *Khadga Mala mantras* are revealed to us. Without meditation we cannot understand a single word. That is why it is so important for *sadhakas* to meditate sincerely and regularly.

We also have to accept the words of scientists who have done research on any subject. One scientist in his research on *Chaitanya,* supreme Consciousness, came to the conclusion that it can only be spoken of in the singular. We can speak of *Chaitanya,* but not *Chaitanyas.* He said that it follows that whatever we see in this universe is nothing but oneness, for only one exists! So you see that there is no duality at all. One Consciousness alone exists. And that *Chaitanya* projects itself first as the prime triangle, and subsequently as all the lines and triangles in the *Sri Chakra,* which is the universe. When we see differences, we are in illusion. Indians call this *maya*.

Every religion speaks about Truth. *Sri Vidya* says that there are no boundaries or limitations for Truth—it is boundless, and when anyone talks about Truth, be it a

---

[22] *Lalitā Sahasranamā,* name 270.

young boy or an elderly person, it is acceptable. In *Sri Vidya,* Bharata is described as a great culture, not an ordinary land. It is often thought that *Bharatiyas,* the people of India, have some blind beliefs. They do not hold blind beliefs. Their beliefs are based on the knowledge of Truth.

According to *Sri Vidya,* Bharata is nothing but Truth. This land did not have any political boundaries. Due to a political fever widespread among people today, we now have boundaries, but the real Bharata cannot be confined to these political boundaries. This is the sacred land where the ancient *rishis* taught about the inner life—not the external life, but the inner light of the Soul. They spread the knowledge of this divine light to the whole world. Bharata is itself that infinite light of the *Atman.* It is vaster than the sky and greater than the oceans. It cannot be limited or controlled by any laws.

The *Vedas* give great importance to human beings. They also have unshakable faith in the natural inner purity of humanity. We often think of ourselves as very inferior and unworthy. We think we are sinners. But the *Vedas* give us a very high position because we have emerged from the supreme source of energy, and are therefore no different from the *bindu*. So the *Vedas* declare, "O man! You are pure; you are purity itself. You are the ether, air, fire, water and earth—you are all the *pancha bhutas,* the five elements. You embody the entire universe! You are part and parcel of that Consciousness. You have come to the Earth for a particular purpose and you are simply a traveler here."

The *Vedas* then proceed to tell us how we should behave in the world. "Do not be unfair, always be fair. Do not be cunning or cheat others. Always be true and pure and practice the *yoga* of meditation. Never forget God." They awaken us with an inspiring call: "You are not an ordinary being—you are the fire which purifies everything. You have been blessed not only with a body, but also with a good mind and intellect. You are the only being with the power to think.

"You are not aware of the power of your will. If you make a strong *sankalpa,* a firm resolve, there is nothing in this world you cannot achieve. Success is easy for you to attain."

The words of the *Vedas* are true. Purity is our nature, but it is covered by ignorance. We need to remove this ignorance through *sadhana.* The *Vedas* hold the human being in high esteem. We must first rise to that level. Then we can go higher still and transcend to God—we *must* merge into the supreme Consciousness from which we emerged.

The *Vedas* give us beautiful universal prayers. They do not speak of any particular sect or religion. Their vision is wide as the sky! One of these prayers is: *"Sarve sukhinah santu."* We always chant, *"Lokah samastah sukhino bhavantu."* Both these *mantras* have the same meaning. They are a beautiful blessing for all creation: "May all beings in the entire creation be happy." The prayer is not just for human beings, it is for all creatures. The next *mantra* is: *"Sarve santu niramaya:* May everyone be free from worries and problems; may no one suffer from pain or disease." The prayer continues: *"Sarve bhadrani pashyantu:* May everyone encounter only auspiciousness; may all beings always prosper and succeed in their endeavors." Such is the generous feeling and wish of the *Vedas* for all the beings in the universe.

Om asato mā sad gamaya
Tamaso mā jyotir gamaya
Mṛtyor mā amṛtam gamaya

Om śānti śānti śāntiḥ

Lokāḥ samastāḥ sukhino bhavantu 3x

ॐ

KAVACHA DEVI: THE SHIELD OF PROTECTION

Embodiment of Divine Souls, Amma's Most Beloved Children,

The *bindu trikona shloka,* which is a prime *shloka* in *Sri Vidya,* starts with a prayer that says the entire universe originates from the *bindu,* which is in the *Sri Chakra.* From this *bindu sthana,* which represents supreme Consciousness, emerges the first *trikona,* or triangle, in the *Sri Chakra.* Each side of this first triangle represents one of the sacred seed syllables, *Aim, Srim,* and *Hrim.* These sacred seed syllables are the subtle forms of the three prime *shaktis*—Maha Lakshmi, Maha Saraswati and Maha Kali.

Innumerable triangles form from this triangle; the entire cosmos comes from the *bindu sthana* of *Sri Chakra,* which is *Omkara* itself. The *trishula,* Lord Siva's trident, is in the shape of a triangle. There are many shapes in nature, such as the bud of the lotus flower, which also resemble the original triangle from which all forms in the universe unfold.

In our morning talk, we spoke of these points, and how we enter into *maya,* delusion, by seeing the *trikona* that emerges from the *bindu* as different from supreme Consciousness itself. Now we will discuss the *Kavacha Devi mantra* in *Khadga Mala.*

If we believe that everything we see is real, that itself is *maya. Maya* is subtle. But when you can see or believe in that which is unseen—in the power behind whatever we are seeing here—then, it has been said, you are beginning to understand the true nature of creation. That is where *Sri Vidya* starts.

Before creation, what was there? How can that indivisible Consciousness—the *parama jyoti* we have been discussing—be described?

Omkara, the *Pranava nada* or primordial sound, is just light—that's all it is. And that light never ever had movement; it was inanimate, just silently there. That indivisible Consciousness is called *nishchala jyoti.* It is very constant and very still, without any movement at all. In the *Vedas,* that *jyoti,* or light—that *prakasha*, or effulgence—is also called *Svayam Bhagavati.* It is very still. But then the radiance of the *trikona,* the triangle, emerged from that *nishchala jyoti* with *Aim, Srim* and *Hrim.* From *Aim,* sound was formed; from *Srim*, light was formed; and from *Hrim,* energy was formed. That is how creation started from the *Sri Chakra.*

We are all struggling very hard on the spiritual path to reach the final destination. But first we need to clear some obstacles and dust covering our *chakras* before we can progress. This dust is nothing but the *samskaras* of this birth and previous births. In each and every birth, the acts we have done have accumulated as *samskaras,* and that's what is covering the *chakras*. So we need a lot of *sadhana*; effort is very important. When we meditate and do *sadhana,* this *chakra* dust slowly, gradually clears. Then the *chakras* regain their lost glory and glow very brightly. The *mantra* that causes these clouds to be cleared is *Kavacha Devi Mantra*. When a *sadhaka* is trying to reach the final state, the very name of *Kavacha Devi* has the tremendous power to help us remove the dust from our *chakras*.

In the process of *sadhana,* we need a lot of help, and we need grace. Grace is so important! When the Divine has graced us, only then can we sit and meditate correctly, take proper guidance and proceed in our *sadhana* without interruption. With the effort of daily practicing meditation in our *sadhana,* the *kundalini* energy in the *muladhara chakra* is awakened, and slowly, from one *chakra* to the next, it begins to ascend. We can bring it all the way up to the *ajna chakra*—the *chakra* between the eyebrows. When it reaches there, which itself is very, very great, we enter *savikalpa samadhi.* In this state, we are still not completely absorbed in meditation; there is still some body consciousness.

In some people, when the *kundalini* reaches the *ajna chakra*, it suddenly drops down, bringing them back to normal consciousness. We must go further upward, but it is not that easy. In the secret knowledge of *Sri Vidya,* it is said that *Kavacha Devi* is the one who helps us when we have reached the *savikalpa samadhi* state. *Kavacha Devi* helps us ascend to the *sahasrara* and enter the *nirvikalpa samadhi* state. In that state, there is no sense of identity at all: you are completely absorbed in the *Atman;* you are in bliss, without any body consciousness. Whenever anyone meditates and reaches that state, even a beginner, *Kavacha Devi* will protect that *sadhaka,* or aspirant, in the form of light.

Actually the very word *kavacha* means armor, a shield of protection. *Kavacha Devi* is a form of Divine Mother. When we do *sadhana,* this light or radiance is always protecting us as a *kavacha,* an armor, around us. As we succeed in our meditation—as the *kundalini* rises—we will slowly proceed upward through the *chakras*, without ever slipping back. That is the protection we get from *Kavacha Devi*.

When people are completely immersed in this world, involved in worldly activities, they do not have the quality of radiance at all. They do not have an aura of light. But when you are practicing meditation, practicing *yoga,* radiance will always be surrounding and enveloping you. And this radiance will increase, the fragrance will increase as you proceed in your *sadhana*.

Kavacha Devi has another name in the *Khadga Mala*. She is called *Vighneshwari*. *Vighneshwara* is Lord Ganesha, or *Ganapati*. He is the one who removes all the obstacles in our life—you know about that. Whatever *vighnas,* or obstacles, we have, He removes them all with His *shakti*. There are *shad vikaras,* six inner enemies or vices, which cause problems for the *sadhaka*. Sometimes we advance; sometimes we stop and come back to the same place we started. This happens because we are overcome by the *shad vikaras,* the six inner enemies. But when we sincerely practice *sadhana, Kavacha Devi* protects us and sees that all these *vighnas,* obstacles, in the form of the *shad vikaras,* the six inner enemies, are removed. So, according to *Sri Vidya,* that is why *Kavacha Devi* is also called *Vighneshwari*, the one who removes all the *vighnas,* all the obstacles in the spiritual path.

Who is greatest in *Sri Vidya* or *Maha Vidya?* It is none other than Lord Siva Himself. That's why Lord Siva has also been praised as the *Parama Guru,* the supreme *Guru,* the greatest of all the *Gurus*, the greatest teacher. That's the reason why we also praise Him as *Dakshinamurti,* the form in which He imparts the greatest knowledge of this *Maha Vidya*.

So here at this retreat, we are discussing the greatest *vidya,* the greatest education of all, this *Maha Vidya,* this *Sri Vidya*. Now the question may arise, "What shall we do when we go home? Do we have to be immersed in meditation all the time? Do we have to be doing constant *sadhana?"*

You each have duties you have to attend to. Many of you are householders, some of you have to work, and some of you are still struggling to be educated. Children, you do not have to give up all your responsibilities and only do *sadhana*. Whatever your *dharma* is, you have to do that. You cannot completely give up the responsibilities you already have. You can continue to go to your office, do business and be in family life—but be unattached and always contemplating on supreme Divinity.

Always try to meditate—practice meditation every day. Meditate for as many hours as you possibly can. Give a lot of importance to meditation in your life, for when you do meditation daily, as we have already mentioned, *Kavacha Devi's kavacha,* armor, will always surround you. Rays of this radiance will be around you all the time, and your meditation will be filled with golden light, too. You will be able to handle problems easily and solve them easily too; everything in life goes smoothly for a meditator.

However, meditation has its own problems. As for when we will attain Self-Realization, this depends on one's *sadhana*—how intensely we are doing *sadhana,* how strongly we are doing *sadhana,* how sincerely we are doing *sadhana.* The highest attainment depends on that. But we should not give up hope. There is always hope. If we continue to practice meditation regularly, we will surely succeed.

Amma sings:

Jananī jananī jagat kāriṇī mā
Oṁkāriṇī mā paripūraṇī mā
Paripūraṇī mā annapūraṇī mā
Jananī jananī jagat kāriṇī mā

Śiva śakti mayī trailokya mayī
Catur veda mayī pañca bhūta mayī
Ṣad cakra mayī sapta loka mayī
Jananī jananī jagat kāriṇī mā

Aṣṭa lakṣmī mayī nava cakra mayī
Nava ratna mayī nava bīja mayī
Nava padma mayī nava rāga mayī
Nava jīva mayī navanīta mayī
Jananī jananī jagat kāriṇī mā

The meaning of this beautiful song is exactly what we have been discussing, in very simple form, here in this retreat. It starts with *"Omkarini,"* praising Divine Mother by saying, "You are nothing but the *Omkara,* the supreme Light, which is *purna,* complete, with absolutely no division at all." As we have discussed, this is the point from which the *bindu* expands, starting with the *trikona,* the triangle of the *Aim, Srim and Hrim bijaksaras*. From there *Siva Shaktimayi,* that effulgence, simply manifests Itself in innumerable different forms.

When supreme Consciousness can perform the wonders of creating this mysterious universe, then it is not impossible for that Consciousness to assume form too. It assumed the form of Siva Shakti, which became the *Chatur Vedas,* the four *Vedas,* and then the *pancha bhutas.* After the *pancha bhutas,* It became the six *chakras.* Gradually, It divided further and assumed innumerable different forms, with different meanings. All this is explained in the song: how Consciousness divided into celestial beings like the *Ashta Lakshmis*—the eight forms of Maha Lakshmi Devi, the seven celestial regions, and gradually, all manifestations. The source for all this is that *Omkara*. That's why we start the song with *Omkarini ma*. This is such a beautiful song; it contains the entire meaning of *Sri Vidya!*

Om śānti śānti śāntiḥ

ॐ

SRI LALITA SAHASRANAMA: MOST POWERFUL SHASTRA[23]

Embodiments of Divine Souls, Amma's Most Beloved Children,

We have been discussing the three forms mentioned in *Sri Vidya. Omkara* is *Ishwara,* who Himself is absolute silence. He is *Dakshinamurti.*[24] The divine *Omkara* is also Shakti. That Siva and Shakti imparted the knowledge of *Sri Vidya* to teach people about the *brahmanda,* the universe.

It is truly wonderful that *Dakshinamurti* teaches about the cosmos, the universes and the *brahmandas,* because we do not know about *brahmanda,* or even about Mother Earth. The essence of the Earth, the essence of the universe, the essence of the cosmos, is Siva and Shakti—the entire universe is only the combination of Siva and Shakti. And what is the meaning of *vidya* in this world—what is real education? Education is understanding this *brahmanda*. In *Sri Vidya,* we want to see that light hidden in all the plants and flowers, and each and every leaf.

So if we want true education, that is, *Brahma Vidya, Yoga Vidya, Maha Vidya,* we have to pray to Lord *Dakshinamurti*. He is the *Guru,* the *Parama Guru*—supreme *Guru*—of all the *Gurus*. He maintains silence, absolute silence. In silence He teaches *Brahma Vidya. Om*

---

[23] *Śāstra:* (instruction, textbook) The *Vedas* and other holy scriptures, including law books and commentaries.

[24] *Dakṣiṇāmūrtī*: (*dakṣiṇa*: south + *mūrtī*: form or image) The form that faces south. In ancient times, Lord Siva manifested as a youth in this form. He taught in silence under a tree, initiating and guiding even elder sages. He taught his disciples by direct transmission of spiritual energy.

is the cause. *Kameshwara Brahma Vidya, Kameshwara prana nadi*[25]*:* divine light always dwells in *Kameshwara,* Lord Siva. So *Dakshinamurti* is the real teacher, the real *Guru* for all the *Gurus* who are mentioned in *Sri Vidya*. The first *Guru* in *Sri Vidya* is *Dakshinamurti*, Lord Siva Himself, because He is the one who is said to be the greatest *Sri Vidya upasaka,* or worshipper, and He is the one who has taught the *Sri Vidya upasana* to everyone in this world.

Here in these sacred mountains, Guru Gautama, Lopamudra—the wife of Agastya Muni—and Guru Vasishtha meditated for one thousand years. You can walk in the forests where they walked, and sit by the beautiful ponds where they meditated. In the evening they are walking here. So all the trees are *vishuddha*—supremely pure—trees, all the stones are *vishuddha* stones, and all the mountains are *vishuddha* mountains, because *Omkara* is in these mountains. You can pray, "O beloved mountain, you are a very sacred mountain, a very powerful and pure mountain! All the *rishis* meditated in your lap. Please bless me with the highest development of Consciousness, in meditation in your lap."

Śrī vidyām jagatām dhātrīm sṛṣṭi sthiti layeśvarī
Namāmi lalitām nityām mahā tripura sundarī

Yā devī sarva bhūteṣu śakti rūpeṇa samsthitā
Namastasyai namastasyai namastasyai namo namaḥ

Among all the *puras,* cities, the *Sri pura*—also known as *Manidwipa,* the dwelling place of Divine Mother in the form of Maha Lakshmi Devi—stands as the supreme one. And out of all the *sahasranamas*, the thousand names we have for each of the Gods and Goddesses, *Sri Lalita*

---

[25] *Lalitā Sahasranāma,* name 373. Divine Mother is the *prāna,* vital energy, that flows through Kameshwara, Lord Siva.

Sahasranama is said to be the greatest of all. Why is this so? Why is it so powerful? We will be discussing that today.

In *Sri Vidya*, the *Lalita Sahasranama* is mentioned very extensively. It is the greatest *shastra*, and very important in *Sri Vidya*. Each and every one of the thousand names in *Lalita Sahasranama* is a *mantra*. *Kulamritaika rasika* is the ninetieth *mantra,* and begins the *Yoga Vidya* or *Maha Vidya* section of *Lalita Sahasranama,* which speaks about the greatest *yoga* and greatest philosophy.

In the *Sri Suktam* we also come across this. The thirteenth and fourteenth *shlokas* of *Sri Suktam* speak about the sun and moon and *nadis,* channels within us. Actually, according to some *Vedas* there is a little bit of interchange here and there in the *Sri Suktam,* and sometimes the fourteenth *shloka* becomes the thirteenth and the thirteenth becomes the fourteenth. In the version that we chant, when we do the *Samputita Sri Suktam,* first comes the *shloka* that mentions *chandra,* or the moon. In our bodies, we have the sun, the moon and all the elements. The *ida* and *pingala* are *nadis,* or passages, through which we take in the breath; the *ida* corresponds with the moon, and the *pingala nadi* with the sun.

Chandra, the moon, represents the mind. The mind is always active; it is the cause of all the obstructions we have in our *sadhana*. If we are to succeed in our *sadhana,* first the mind has to subside; it must become completely still. Only when the mind becomes inactive can the intellect become active. In the process of *pranayama* we regulate our breathing system through the *ida* and *pingala*. *Pranayama* quiets the mind and leads to the awakening of the *kundalini*. This is very important in *sadhana,* and has to be done properly. It is this we are chanting about in these two *shlokas* of *Sri Suktam.*

The 90th to 96th *mantras* of *Sri Lalita Sahasranama* speak about the *yoga* of *kundalini.* These beautiful *mantras* are:

Kulāmritaika rasikā Kula saṅketa pālinī
Kulāṅganā Kulāntasthā Kaulinī Kula yoginī Akulā

The science of *mantra* here explains how the *kundalini* energy, which is sleeping in the *muladhara chakra,* gets awakened. This greatest *vidya* narrates what the *kundalini* is, where it is located, how many petals there are in the *chakras*, their colors, what is contained in each *chakra*, and how they can be awakened. In these *mantras* is the secret of *kundalini yoga.*

The *mantras* that follow are:

Samayāntasthā Samayācāra tatparā.

Samayachara and *vamachara* are two types of *puja,* or worship. Adi Shankaracharya[26] has mentioned *samayachara puja.* According to him, what is it? It is nothing but *Yoga Vidya!* The meditation we are doing is itself *samaya puja. Samaya puja* is a *sattvic puja,* where the individual is established in the inner world—all *puja* is done inwardly. Our normal *puja* is external worship; we bring flowers or other offerings to the lotus feet of the Divine. But in *samaya puja,* or inward worship, the seven lotuses in the form of the *chakras* open and bloom, and they are the beautiful flowers that we offer as we reach the *sahasrara*, the thousand petal lotus. *Samaya puja* is the correct way to approach Mother Divine.

---

[26]*Ādi Śankarāchārya:* (788-820 AD) Considered to be an incarnation of Lord Siva, this saint has over 300 literary works to his credit. He also led the 7th Century Hindu revival. He established *maths,* monasteries at the four corners of India, which maintain an unbroken lineage. The officiating pontiff of each of these *maths* is called " Shankaracharya" even today.

Going further, the 100th *mantra* of *Sri Lalita Sahasranama* is *Brahma granthi vibhedini. Brahma granthi* is a knot—an obstruction within us that prevents the *kundalini* from rising. But when we do *sadhana,* the *kundalini* in the *muladhara* pierces or releases the knot of the *Brahma granthi* and then rises to the other *chakras*.

The *svadhishthana chakra* is not mentioned here. *Manipurantarudita* is the next *mantra,* referring to the *manipura chakra;* the knot here is the *Vishnu granthi*. When this knot is released, the *kundalini shakti* then reaches the *ajna chakra—Ajna chakrantaralastha.* The *Rudra granthi* is at the *ajna chakra,* and is also released through *sadhana*.

So from the 90th *mantra* in *Sri Lalita Sahasranama,* starting with:

Kulāmṛtaika rasikā kula saṅketa pālinī
Kulāṅganā Kulāntasthā Kaulinī Kula yoginī

and going through the 111th *mantra, kundalini yoga* is spoken about in great detail in code form. The *mantras* do not mention all the *chakras,* but only those where the three *granthis* or knots are located. So we have:

Mulādhāraika nilayā Brahma graṅthi vibhedinī

The *Brahma granthi,* the knot of Brahma, is located at the *muladhara chakra.*

Maṇipurāṅta ruḍitā Viṣṇu graṅthi vibhedinī

The *Vishnu granthi* is at the *manipura chakra.* And

Ājñā cakrāṅtarālasthā Rudra graṅthi vibhedinī

The *Rudra granthi* is at the *ajna chakra*.

The *svadhishthana chakra,* just above the *muladhara,* the *anahata* or heart *chakra,* and the *vishuddhi* or throat *chakra* are not mentioned.

These *granthis,* knots, are not that easy to break through. They are composed of an individual's *samskaras,* which are very hard to release. The *kundalini,* which awakens in the *muladhara,* sometimes cannot pass through them. So in *Sri Lalita Sahasranama,* in *Sri Vidya,* the method to release these knots which obstruct our progress is mentioned very specifically: they can be released by the grace of Divine Mother.

And what happens after *Ajna chakrantaralastha Rudra granthi vibhedini?* After the *Rudra granthi* is released, the *kundalini* can rise through the channel of the *sushumna nadi* and reach the *sahasrara*, the crown *chakra:*

Sahasrār āmbujāruḍhā

When it reaches the *sahasrara,* what happens?

Sudhāsārābhi varṣiṇī

When the energy reaches the crown *chakra,* which is *Brahmaikya stithi*—the merging of the individual personality, *atman,* with the universal Personality, *Brahman*—the individual becomes the supreme Self! Then, *Sudhasarabhi varshini:* we'll be drenched in that nectar, that radiance—completely flooded in that flow of elixir of divine bliss. That is what happens in *Brahmaikya stithi*. For this we need intense *sadhana,* with a lot of *tapas*, austerity, and meditation. When we do such *sadhana,* we will surely attain the state of *Brahmaikya stithi*.

After *Sudhasarabhi varshini,* the next *mantra,* 107, in *Sri Lalita Sahasranama* is:

Taḍillatā sama ruciḥ

The *kundalini* is awakened according to the intensity of our *sadhana,* our degree of inwardness, and the control we have over the lower natures. This beautiful *mantra* says the rise of the *kundalini* through the *sushumna* channel to the *sahasrara* is like a flash of lightning.

There is a difference between the *granthis* and the *chakras*. The *chakras* are the invisible energy centers in our body, whereas the *granthis* or knots are different stages we must transcend and release through our *sadhana.* First *Sri Lalita Sahasranama* speaks about the *granthis—Brahma granthi, Vishnu granthi* and *Rudra granthi*—then about the energy of *kundalini,* which is like lightning.

In the next *mantra,* the six *chakras* are mentioned again:

Ṣad cakropari saṁsthitā

When the *kundalini* transcends the six *chakras*, it finally reaches the *sahasrara,* where it glows in glorious effulgence. The following *mantra* is:

Mahā Śakti

Maha Shakti is the greatest of all the energies in the world. *Maha Shakti* is nothing but the *kundalini* after it reaches the *sahasrara.*

There is a connection between one *mantra* and the next. After *Maha Shakti,* the 110th *mantra* is:

Kuṅḍalinī

And then the 111th *mantra* is:

Bisa taṅtu tanīyasī

From the *muladhara chakra,* through the channel of the *sushumna nadi, kundalini* ascends from one *chakra* to the next, and finally reaches the *sahasrara*. So from the 90th *mantra* to the 111th *mantra, Sri Lalita Sahasranama* speaks about *kundalini yoga.*

After this, the next section begins with the 112th *mantra:*

Bhavānī.

Om asato mā sad gamaya
Tamaso mā jyotir gamaya
Mṛtyor mā amṛtam gamaya

Om śānti śānti śāntiḥ

Lokāḥ samastāḥ sukhino bhavantu 3x

ॐ

THE FIVE SHARIRAS, BODIES

Śrī vidyām jagatām dhātrīm sṛṣṭi sthiti layeśvarīm
Namāmi lalitām nityām mahā tripura sundarīm

Yā devī sarva bhūteṣu śakti rūpeṇa samsthitā
Namastasyai namastasyai namastasyai namo namaḥ

Children,

In the morning session we discussed the references to *kundalini* in *Sri Lalita Sahasranama*. The *Lalita Sahasranama* is part of *Sri Vidya*. We very briefly discussed the names from 90 to 111, which speak about the *kundalini*. These names from *Kulamritaika rasika* to *Maha shakti, kundalini,* and *Bisa tantu taniyasi* have hidden in them a wonderful *yogic* description of *kundalini shakti*. The subject of *kundalini* as described in *Sri Vidya* is a vast one and would take years to cover.

Lalita Sahasranama has given all the details about all the *yogas*. It describes, for example, all of the *chakras* and their formation, the form and color of the *chakras,* and it also describes the power and latent energy in that *chakra*. All this has been described in great detail in *Sri Vidya*. [Amma holds up a picture.]

This picture shows Divine Mother holding Lord Ganesha in Her lap. This is nothing but the *muladhara chakra* which they have depicted as Divine Mother holding Lord Ganesha. Yes, *muladhara chakra* is Mother; Ganesha is *kundalini*. [Amma laughs]

The presiding deity of the *muladhara chakra* is Lord Ganesha, as we know, and that form of *kundalini* is depicted so beautifully in this picture as Divine Mother holding Lord Ganesha in Her lap. When you meditate on *kundalini* in the *muladhara chakra*, imagine Divine Mother seated there with Ganesha in Her lap.

In *Sri Vidya*, in the chapter on *kundalini,* we learn about the five bodies or *shariras* we all have:

1. *Annamayam*
2. *Prāṇamayam*
3. *Manomayam*
4. *Vijnāṇamayam*
5. *Ānandamayam*

1. Annamaya sharira: The physical body, which is nourished and sustained by *anna,* food. This body is composed of the *pancha bhutas,* the five elements. Everything in this world grows due to the first energy—*Surya agni*—the fire of the sun, which we can see with our eyes as light, and which also produces heat. Without the rays of the sun there would be no life at all, no agriculture. Nature herself is cooking the food, that is, making it ripe. Moonbeams are needed for the formation of leaves and seeds. So here we are discussing the energy of light, which is the prime energy necessary for the growth and maintenance of the gross body.

2. Pranamaya sharira: The subtle body, composed of *prana,* vital energy. Solar energy is needed to activate this subtle body. The gross body, which is nourished by food, also needs this vital *pranic* energy within to sustain it. One who has a strong *pranamaya sharira* is never lazy or depressed. He is always active and energetic.

3. Manomaya sharira: The mental body. It is very important for a spiritual aspirant to have a strong mind. Some people are strong physically but are very weak mentally. At times, they cannot face and handle the problems of life. They experience fear or get depressed, which causes them to become overwhelmed, experience numbness or a kind of inertia, and lose interest in everything.

All of you have already noticed that here in India, poor people have no comforts or facilities. They work very hard but still they don't have proper homes, enough food, and so on. But you can see a cheerfulness and happiness in the faces of these people. They do constant *japa,* chanting sacred *mantras* all the time. Although they do not possess much externally, they are content and happy because they are always in contemplation. They have a sound mental body and are not under the influence of depression at all.

Mentally, we have to be very strong. When the mental body is strong, the physical body is also strong. It is particularly important for the aspirant to have a very strong and powerful mental body. The *manomaya sharira* gets energized through *mantra* repetition and meditation.

4. *Vijnanamaya sharira:* The intellectual body. This body is capable of going beyond the intellect, too. The *vijnanamaya sharira* is greater than the mental body. When we are initiated into *Sri Vidya,* we are initiated into various forms of intense *sadhana,* such as the sacred and powerful *Gayatri Mantra.* When one is meditating, one's whole brain system is energized. It is filled with the bright effulgence of divine light, and this strengthens our *vijnanamaya sharira.* We need a strong intellect to discriminate between right and wrong, and between the transitory and the eternal.

5. *Anandamaya sharira:* The body of eternal bliss. This is the body in which the *sadhaka* will be completely established in that Oneness, in absolute peace, in *Sat svarupa,* Truth. One will be in this blissful state all the time, always immersed in the bliss of identifying with the Divine. It is here that you realize that you yourself are the

supreme Soul in the form of *Chaitanya,* as we were discussing yesterday.

When we practice regular *sadhana* and meditate daily, we finally reach the *sahasrara.* We merge into the eternal effulgence of the supreme Soul, which is nothing but *Omkara!*

Every individual has these five bodies. An ordinary person with no spiritual inclination will always be stuck at the lower level, in the gross body, the *annamaya sharira. Sri Vidya* makes us aware that we have not come to this world to keep identifying with the physical body. We need to go beyond the *annamaya sharira* and transcend through the *pranamayam* to *manomayam,* and from *vijnanamayam,* finally, to the fifth and final *anandamaya sharira*. We need to evolve spiritually and be established in the beautiful body of supreme, eternal bliss!

We have talked about some of the *mantras* in the *Lalita Sahasranama* that speak about *kundalini* and this great *kundalini yoga*.

There are also some *mantras* that speak about the secrets of that subtle energy, of that supreme Consciousness. *Niradhara upasana,* worship of the formless aspect of God, is described in the *mantras* 132-155, from *Niradhara* and ending *Nirishvara.* It is common for people to worship the *murti* or form of God. But *Lalita Sahasranama* speaks about the *nirguna upasana,* which is meditation itself, where we are worshipping the formless aspect, the Supreme without attributes. The names in this section extol the unimaginable, magnificent *nirguna* nature of supreme Consciousness, which is devoid of attributes and qualities. *Mantras* 85-89:

Śrīmad vāgbhava kuṭaika svarūpa muka paṅkajā ...
Mūla kūṭa traya kaḷebarā

These names discuss the secrets of subtle energy, the power and form of *mantra,* and the *mantra chaitanya,* the consciousness in the *mantra.*

Mantras 990-999 and 1000:

Abhyāsātiśaya jñātā....... Śiva Śaktyaika rūpiṇī
Śrī Lalitāmbikā

These names contain the very essence of *Sri Vidya.* They speak of the final merging of the individual soul with the supreme Soul, where there is no duality at all.

All the thousand *mantras* in the *Sri Lalita Sahasranama* can be grouped into sixteen divisions. Each division or section contains innumerable secrets. We can only give a few hints and key words here and there about all the secrets embedded in *Sri Lalita Sahasranama.* You have been given the numbers, too—now you have to study for yourselves and find out. [Laughter]

All these days, many of you have been chanting *Lalita Sahasranama* and experiencing the energy of the *mantras.* Children, *Lalita Sahasranama* is not just a book of recitation—one has to have a basis of meditation to understand the *namas,* the *mantras.* This is because it is a *yoga vidya*—it contains the knowledge of all the *yogas;* it is a *mantra shastra,* a holy book of *mantras;* and it is beyond all the *shastras. Sahasranamas* are the thousand names in praise of a particular God or Goddess. For each and every God or Goddess, there are *sahasranamas,* like *Agni Sahasranama, Saraswati Sahasranama, Vishnu Sahasranama, Siva Sahasranama,* and so on. But only the *sahasranama* for Mother Divine, *Sri Lalita Sahasranama,* is known as the *Rahasya Sahasranama. "Rahasya"* means "secret." The thousand names of Mother Divine are secret. To understand the deep inner meanings hidden in the divine names in *Sri Lalita Sahasranama,* you need a strong foundation of meditation. All the *rahasyas,* secrets, will be revealed to you in meditation.

As we meditate and then recite the *Lalita Sahasranama,* we can understand the meanings which are hidden in the *Lalita Sahasranama*. We have discussed some *mantras* here and there, those that deal with *kundalini,* and the *nirguna upasana,* and also the *Siva Shaktyaikya rupini mantra,* where the individual soul merges in the universal Soul. *Sri Lalita Sahasranama* shows the way for an individual to proceed on the path of *Sri Vidya*: how to do our *sadhana,* and how we can merge with that universal Personality. The last ten *mantras,* from 990 up to 1,000, speak about merging into that Absolute, where the *sadhaka,* or aspirant, becomes merged into that oneness, and no longer remembers the individual self.

Sri Lalita Sahasranama speaks of all of this, and that is why it is the greatest *sahasranama*. So it is an important part of *Sri Vidya,* where daily the *Sri Vidya* practitioner has to meditate upon the *Pancha Dashakshari Mantra,* chant *Sri Lalita Sahasranama,* and then perform the *Sri Chakra archana*.

ॐ

SRI VIDYAM SHLOKA

Children,

Once the two powerful *rishis,* Sanaka and Sanandana, went to Kailasa to approach Lord Siva and clear their doubts. The Lord gave them *darshan* in the form of *Sri Dakshinamurti,* who is seated on the southern side of Mt. Kailasa. *Dakshinamurti,* a beautiful form of Siva, means Siva who faces the south. The *rishis* offered their humble salutations and asked the Lord, "There are innumerable *yoga vidyas,* according to the philosophies of the different schools. Please tell us, which *vidya* is the source, basis and origin of all these *yoga vidyas?*"

In answer, Lord Siva chanted the *shloka* which we have been chanting here daily. He said:

Śrī vidyām jagatām dhātrīm sṛṣṭi sthiti layeśvarīm
Namāmi lalitām nityām mahā tripura sundarīm

Divine Mother, the Mother of the whole universe, is the cause of the creation, sustenance and dissolution of the universe. The answer is to be found in Sri Vidya only.

That is how this *shloka* originated. When we chant this *shloka,* we might think it is just a verse in praise of Mother Divine, mentioning Her various aspects. But when Lord Siva answered the *rishis'* question, He started with the words *"Sri Vidya."* So the secret of the answer is *Sri Vidya.*

Lord Siva continued:

Jagatam dhatrim: Sri Vidya is Divine Mother, Mother of the whole universe.

Srishti sthiti layeshwari: She is the cause of its creation, sustenance and dissolution.

Namami Lalitam nityam maha tripura sundari: She is the eternal form who is praised as *Lalita,* and also as *Maha Tripura Sundari.*

This *shloka* is His full answer to their question, but the answer, literally, is in the first words: *Sri Vidyam.* The basis, source and origin of all the *yoga vidyas* in the world, whichever *yoga* you read about or practice, is *Sri Vidya* only.

The next question the *rishis* asked was, "What is *vidya?* How can we implement it in our lives?"

Lord Siva replied, *"Sri Vidya* is *jnana aishvaryam,* the priceless treasure of true knowledge. *Jnana* means to know the unknown and see the unseen!"

For example, we see a tree. If we think about a tree; we know that it has a trunk and lots of roots, and so on. But what is the energy that makes it live? What is the origin of this tree? When we try to think more deeply about this, we don't find an answer. In the same way, we may think about a mountain, and wonder who created this mountain, how did it come to be there? What is behind all the countless names and forms we see in this world? The same question can be asked about human beings. We may know the history, the physiology of human beings, but our knowledge does not go beyond that. There is a limit to all our knowledge, beyond which we do not know the answer.

Let us take our world. We are on Mother Earth. Everything happens in a very organized manner. The seasons—summer, rainy season and winter—follow each other. Plants grow according to these seasons and give us food, and so on. Who created this world and organized everything so well? What is the cause? To know the answers to these questions is real *jnana.* The physical sciences give us superficial knowledge. We need deep knowledge, the knowledge of the reality behind everything. This is *jnana.*

To attain *jnana* a seeker needs to immerse himself in intense *sadhana*—in deep, not superficial, meditation. We will not attain *jnana* by meditating on the surface level.

Let me give you an example: Many travelers were walking along a road. After a while, they came to a large rock. Some went around it, some walked over it, some sat on it and ate their food, some rested on it for awhile and others slept on it. They all saw it only as a big stone. But when a sculptor saw the same rock, he felt respect for it. He never stepped on it because he saw Divinity in the stone. He began to chisel the rock. Day after day he worked with total absorption and finally transformed it into a beautiful image of God! It was no longer just an ordinary rock.

There are different kinds of people in this world. Ordinary people are not creative—they have no imagination. The sculptor had inner vision. He worked with intensity, sincerity and effort. *Shraddha,* strong inclination or desire, is most important. It is very important for us to have sincerity, deep involvement and intensity in our *sadhana*. We should never give up self-effort. We need a strong inclination, a deep desire to merge with God. Without self-effort and total immersion in meditation the goal cannot be attained. The education of *Sri Vidya* gives us true knowledge, but for Self-Realization we need total involvement, immersion and strong desire—we need all three.

The sculptor transformed the lifeless rock into a living image of Divinity! His intense absorption, dedication and loving labor created a form of timeless beauty. On the completion of the statue, when he had carved the open eyes, the sculptor experienced immeasurable *ananda!* Only the sculptor will know what he is experiencing. Even a physician who is deeply involved in a serious case feels great joy when he saves the life of his patient.

We need to be as involved and absorbed in our *sadhana* as the sculptor was in his work of art. Without this dedication, we can never experience supreme bliss. An aspirant has to forget himself and go beyond the ego as well as thoughts. The *Upanishads* tell us:

Ānandam Brahma
Supreme Consciousness is eternal bliss.

When our life is full of commotion it is difficult to experience *ananda*. Our present world is experiencing a lot of commotion. The darkness of ignorance, a sense of insecurity and all kinds of troubles and difficulties are ruling each and every nation of the world today. Society needs peace. The only solution is the answer found in the *Upanishads.* They advise us to turn inward. Peace can only be found through prayer, *yoga* and meditation. Spiritual life alone can bring us the peace and happiness we seek.

Not so long ago, life in India was different. There were no demonic instruments such as telephones and television. [Laughter] There was no electricity either. People lived in villages and worked all day in the fields. They came home at sunset, ate their food and went to sleep. The so-called facilities of modern life are really disadvantages. Before the age of technology, simple people like weavers were happy working all day on their looms, weaving cloth and *saris.* They slept peacefully at night after a hard day's work. Potters made beautiful clay items with their hands; sculptors chiseled stone and created beauty.

The Belur Temple is exquisite. Three generations of artisans worked from sunrise to sunset to complete the living stone figures, perfect in every detail, and the intricate decorative panels and pillars of this unique place of worship. The artisans who carved the images in the temple did not care about money. They were completely dedicated to their work and immersed in it. They found joy and fulfillment in their creative work; they were happy and content. And today, even after 1,000 years, the sculptures are still alive! Some of them appear to be dancing. Siva is dancing there. The ornaments on the statues are so intricate and look so real. These sculptors had no other work, no other distractions. They would just take their food, go to bed and start again the next day.

Those who wrote poems and the *Vedas* had the same kind of dedication. Poets, painters, musicians, dancers and other artists throughout the world lost themselves in their art. Handicrafts were popular. There are still some craftsmen in China and India who make beautiful things with their hands. But slowly we are losing these traditional arts because of the mad race for money.

Competition for riches and success consumes us. The *rakshasi yantras,* demonic instruments which we have "invented," have mercilessly taken away the happiness, contentment and peace from our lives. Life has become so mechanical from morning until night. People are so engaged in work, there is no spare time for the family. There are people who don't even speak with the family members in their house, they have so much work to do! All these things are happening. We are living in an age in which we have to buy water. Some people have to buy air, oxygen. No doubt, we will soon be paying for sunlight, too!

The kind of life we lead today has gotten us so absorbed that it makes us very tired. Sometimes we think we need sleep, but what we really need is rest for our minds. We need to change, otherwise we will have to learn many lessons. One day we will get a strong blow, and then we will realize our mistake. Why not wake up and realize it right now? We are running after a mirage in this world. It has made our life a prison. We have poisoned our life by chasing after meaningless, momentary pleasures. Life should be meaningful, peaceful and content.

Whatever education we have received and whatever we have achieved should give us happiness. If this education or learning has not given us happiness, it is not true education at all. The real education is *Sri Vidya*, *Maha Vidya*. It teaches us about the Supreme. Like a loving mother, *Sri Vidya* teaches us how to be always happy and content, and how to experience life as a gift.

If we work hard only for ourselves and forget about other people, it doesn't bring us happiness at all. We think we have made great progress, but this so-called progress has made us selfish and insensitive to the feelings and suffering of others. *Sri Vidya* says that if we are selfless in our life, we will feel happiness and peaceful very easily. That is why again and again the *shastras,* holy books, tell us to practice *nishkama seva,* selfless service. Selflessness brings immediate peace. The easiest way to attain peace is to help others without wanting anything in return.

We are in a world full of commotion. As we come to know what *shanti*, peace, really is, let us be led from this Untruth to Truth, from this unhappiness to happiness, and from this death to immortality.

Om śānti śānti śāntiḥ

ॐ

QUESTIONS FROM SADHAKAS

Om Śuklām baradharam viṣnum
Śaśi varṇam caturbhujam
Prasanna vadanam dhyāyet
Sarva vighnopa śāntaye

Śrī vidyām jagatām dhātrīm sriṣṭi sthiti layeśvarīm
Namāmi lalitām nityām mahā tripura sundarīm

Yā devī sarva bhūteśu śakti rūpeṇa samsthitā
Namastasyai namastasyai namastasyai namo namaḥ

(Chanting of *Samputitā Śrī Suktam*)

Children,

Some of you have asked about the correct method of performing *Sri Lalita Sahasranama parayana.* There are two ways to do this:

1. In the *stotra parayana,* one simply recites the names one after the other without adding *bijaksharas..*
2. In the *namavali parayana,* each divine name is preceded with the *bijaksharas Om, Aim, Hrim, Srim,* and ends with the word *namah.* For example:

Om Aim Hrīm Śrīm Śrī Mātre namaḥ

The *namavali* is chanted when we do *puja,* or worship. When we worship the *Sri Chakra* or a *Devi murti,* an image of Mother Divine, a flower or a little *kumkum*[27] is offered with the repetition of each Devi name.

---

[27]*kumkum:* An auspicious red powder used in *pūjās*, or ritual worship. It is made by mixing turmeric and lime powder.

Nanna, we need not do the *namavali* daily, but for those who are really interested and have asked this question, they can do the *parayana* of the *stotra* daily, simply reciting the names:

Śrī Māta, Śrī Mahārājnī, Śrīmat Simhāsaneśwarī,

and so on. The *namavali* is done only for *puja.*

The question was asked, "How should we worship the *Sri Chakra?"* If you want to do the *Sri Chakra archana,* or worship, it is good to do it on Fridays, on *pournami,* the day of the full moon, and on other auspicious days such as birthdays. One way is by reciting the *Lalita Sahasranama Namavali* and offering a little *kumkum* with each Devi name. There are several elaborate methods of performing *Sri Chakra puja*. What is most important is that whatever form of *puja* you do should not be performed mechanically, but with intense devotion, complete sincerity, from the very bottom of your heart.

During *homas,* for each and every *mantra* and offering, we say: *Svāhā* .

"Svaha" can be divided into three syllables:

Sva + ā + hā.

Sva means "all that I have, including all my interests," *ā* means "completely," and *hā* means "offering" or "surrendering." So the meaning of *"svaha"* is: "I am offering or surrendering completely all that I have to You, that all-pervasive Almighty." In Sanskrit, another word for *svaha* is *mamekam.* It also means, "I am offering You whatever I have."

These *mantras* are universal prayers. In the *yajnas,* or *vedic* fire ceremonies, the priests chant various *mantras* from the *Vedas*. All these *mantras* are *vedashisha* or *vedashirvada,* the blessings of the *Vedas*. But the people participating in the *homas* often do not know the meaning of all the *mantras.* With the chanting of these sacred *mantras,* the priests are approaching the Almighty or Divinity, and asking that Divinity in various ways for all the things we need in life here on Earth. That is the reason people attend *yajnas.* Just witnessing a *yajna* and listening to the *mantras* is very powerful, as those of you who have participated in *yajnas* know. When we attend a *yajna* ceremony, each and every one who is present receives the blessings of all that has been said in the *Vedas*.

One *vedic mantra* chanted during *yajnas* says: "May I live a hundred years. May I see only good things, hear good things and speak good words for a hundred years. May I not be a slave to anyone. Please bless me to live for one hundred years."

In this beautiful *mantra,* there is deep meaning. It is asking not merely for a hundred years of life spent in bed, but for a life of good health. And why is such a long life being requested?

I am praying not for a hundred years of commotion, but for a life of peace. I am praying to sit near the lotus feet of the revered *Guru* and listen to words of wisdom. That is why I am asking for a life of one hundred years.

During my life, may I speak only good words. And what words are these? Whatever I have heard from *Sri Guru* or my elders, I am praying to share the words of that knowledge with others.

And my final prayer is, "May I never be a slave to anyone, but always be free as a bird." What does that mean? That I should not be under the control of any human being, but a servant only to God. We pray to live like that for a hundred years. This prayer is said on everyone's behalf during *yajnas*. And when it is chanted using the correct meter during the sacred fire ceremony, the vibrations of that chant enter all the people present and make their lives more spiritual.

As everyone here knows, life is not all that easy. Sometimes it is good and at other times it is filled with all kinds of trials and tribulations. There are periods when we suffer from ill-health, or experience depression, financial problems and many other difficulties. There are times when we are completely depleted of mental peace and hope. Losses and problems disturb our mind and speech so that we are unable to think or talk clearly. At such times even intelligent people lose their *viveka,* sense of discrimination, and do not know what they are doing. This can lead to many further problems. The question is, what should we do at such times?

At times like these, we can take refuge in the *Khadga Mala.* We can chant this beautiful *kanti mala,* the luminous garland of the radiance of Mother Divine. This unique chant encompasses the divine forms of both Siva and Shakti in its effulgent rays. It is not merely a fragrant garland of Devi names, but is supreme Light itself! It is clearly stated in the *phala shruti*[28] of the *Khadga Mala* that when we chant this powerful *stotra* with faith and devotion, all our difficulties and losses are destroyed. It is good to chant this in the evening or every Friday. During times of despair and troubles do it once—this is very good.

Many here have asked: "Amma, you have taught us so many things in this Sri Vidya Retreat, including the *Lalita Sahasranama* and the *Khadga Mala Stotra,* but what should we actually do when we go back home? How should we practice this *Sri Vidya* in our daily life?"

The subject of the teachings of *Sri Vidya* is very vast. But the greatest secret of *Sri Vidya* is hidden in the *Khadga Mala*. That is why I am teaching you this sacred and

---

[28] *phala śruti:* (*phala:* fruit) In most *stotras* there are a few verses at the end describing the benefits of chanting that *stotra*. These are known as *phala shruti.*

powerful *stotra*. It is very good to chant the *Khadga Mala* daily. To this, some might say, "We already have so many *mantras!* We have been doing this *mantra,* that *mantra, Sri Suktam* and many, many others. And now Amma is adding one more!" [Laughter]

Nevertheless, if you have time and if you like doing it, you can chant the *Khadga Mala* every evening. It is very beneficial to recite it daily, but if you cannot, do it on Fridays. It is particularly helpful to chant the *Khadga Mala* at least once during times of depression and when faced with other problems. One of the *sadhakas* asked whether the recitation should be done silently or out loud. Whenever we repeat any *stotra,* it has to be chanted out loud.

The *Khadga Mala* is also called *Shakti mala. "Mala"* means "garland." *"Shakti mala"* means "a garland of energy." It is also called *Siva mala,* the garland of Siva. Both Siva and Shakti energies reside eternally in the *Khadga Mala mantras,* so it is a radiant garland entwining Siva and Shakti. Each and every *mantra* in the *Khadga Mala* is nothing but cosmic light and cosmic energy.

The *Khadga Mala* destroys the consequences of all our *prarabdha karmas,* the actions we have performed in past births. It has innumerable powerful *bija mantras.* When you chant these *mantras,* the energy of each and every *mantra* forms a radiant garland around you, which protects you like a shield from all the problems you face. If you chant the *Khadga Mala* regularly, the inner secrets of the *Vedas* and *Upanishads* are gradually revealed to you.

* * * * *

Children, we discussed this earlier today. Imagine a beautiful forest with a path running through it. Many people travel on that path. As they walk along, they come upon an exquisite sculpture by the wayside. They are greatly attracted by its wondrous beauty, and their hearts are filled with joy as they gaze upon it.

Only an artistic person has the eye, the special inner vision, that can create such extraordinary beauty from an ordinary rock. There is something magical in this graceful form that the sculptor has chiseled from stone!

The sculptor is the creator who has carved this beautiful form. Nature is already so beautiful, and the artist has added to its beauty a thousand-fold with his own creative power. The sculptor might create a graceful Lakshmi, a delightful dancing Ganesha, or a serene, meditative Siva reflecting infinite peace. The sculptor's imagination and creative hands infuse life into the forms he creates so that they seem to be alive! They appear to be smiling, laughing and talking! When we look at these incredible sculptures, our hearts are moved, filled with wonder at their entrancing beauty. Only the sculptor has the inner vision and ability to give life to the forms in his imagination.

Ordinary people do not possess this vision. They see all the objects in the world, and they also have a superficial knowledge about them. But there is a light that shines inside every object in this world. We need the inner eye to see that light behind everything in the cosmos. This vision can be attained only through meditation. When you meditate regularly, the inner *chakras* blossom and open. Then you experience that you are not the mind, you are not the intellect, you are beyond everything—you are boundless and supremely free! You are supreme Consciousness!

ॐ

THE BENEFITS OF KHADGA MALA STOTRA

Embodiments of Divine Souls, Amma's Most Beloved Children,

The wrong deeds we have performed in this birth and in previous births become our *prarabdha karma.* They also form our *samskaras,* the deeply-rooted tendencies in our nature. It is not easy to get rid of *prarabdha karmas*. However, the chanting of the *Khadga Mala* destroys millions of *prarabdhas* immediately! That is the power of this divine *Khadga Mala Stotra.* No matter how difficult life may be, or what problems we face, when we recite this powerful *stotra,* immediately we are relieved of all the trials and tribulations we are undergoing. This is so even when previous efforts have failed.

Yeśām vidyā mahā siddhi dāyinī śruti mātrataḥ

One who merely listens to the recitation of this Khadga Mala, which is the essence of Sri Vidya, attains the highest goal.

Siddhi dayini: one will accomplish what one wishes to. All problems are solved, ailments healed, and even the consequences of sins accrued from committing murders or other heinous deeds, as well as *prarabdha karmas,* are all eradicated by the chanting of this sacred and extremely powerful *stotra*. The *sadhaka* is showered with divine grace and all his *sankalpas*, resolves and intentions bear fruit.

Agni vāta mahā kṣobhe rāje rāśṭrasya viplave

The *Khadga Mala* also prevents the destruction of lives and property that result from natural disasters such as volcanoes, thunderstorms, fires and earthquakes. When one chants the *Khadga Mala* at such times, the radiant energy of this powerful *stotra,* like a strong beam of divine light, goes from the person who is chanting to the place where the disaster is occurring and protects everybody. So this beautiful and wonderful *Khadga Mala* can be chanted not only for the benefit of the individual but, in times of upheaval, for the welfare of the king and all the people in the kingdom, for our leaders and everyone in the world.

The *Khadga Mala* is not just a set of names. Each and every *mantra* in the *Khadga Mala* is a source of radiance. You can recite it for yourself as well as for others. If someone is sick, or if a country is having a problem, you can chant this *stotra* and it will help.

The *Khadga Mala* represents the energies in the nine triangles of the *Sri Chakra,* which intersect one another. The whole *Sri Chakra* contains different forms of energy, *Shakti.* Whoever chants the *Khadga Mala stotra* will be blessed by those energies from the *Sri Chakra.*

Ekatra gananā rupo Veda Vedānta gochaḥ:

The glory and significance of the Vedas with their hidden secrets will be revealed to the aspirant who chants Khadga Mala daily. It is even better to chant it as many times as possible.

In addition to the blessings you'll receive from these divine energies and radiance, when you chant *Khadga Mala* at least once in a day, all your *karmas* will be burned away. If you chant it numerous times, the benefit is beyond what words can express.

Khadga Mala is inseparable from its connection with nature and the power to bring balance into nature. Before we chant the *Khadga Mala,* we chant different *bijaksharas* to connect us to the *pancha bhutas. Ram* is for *agni,* fire, *Lam* is for *prithvi,* Mother Earth, *Ham* is *akasha,* space, *Yam* is *vayu,* the wind, and so on. Thus the *pancha bhutas* also become charged with energy, and brought into balance.

ॐ

KHADGA MALA PRAYER SHLOKAS

Nanna,

Sri Vidya talks about *nirguna upasana*—mental worship of formless Consciousness. Meditation is the best form of mental worship. In *nirguna upasana,* we do not worship an image or *murti,* God with form, but come in contact with the light which is Consciousness. The names in *Lalita Sahasranama* from 132, *Niradhara,* to 155, *Nirishwara,* speak about this formless aspect of *Brahman.*

Sri Vidya also gives a lot of importance to the *Khadga Mala.* The subtle secrets of the *Vedas* will be revealed to us like flashes of energy and light when we chant the *Khadga Mala* daily.

Om tādṛśyam khaḍgam āpnoti yena hasta sthitena vai
Aṣṭādaśa mahādvīpā sāmrāḍ bhoktā bhaviṣyati

Tadrishyam khadgam apnoti: There is nothing equal to the *Khadga Mala* in this world.

Yena hasta sthitena vai: The *Khadga Mala* itself is light and energy, and burns away *samskaras.* We want to experience *akhanda Brahmananda,* supreme Bliss, and be established in that state forever. The *sadhaka* who reaches the state of *maha nirvana* will have no rebirth at all. This state can be attained while still in the body. Once we reach that state, we will be completely unattached to whatever we do. The *sadhaka* becomes a knower of *sarva agama rahasya,* that is, the mysteries contained in the revealed scriptures.

Ashtadasa mahadwipa: All the planets, galaxies, all creation. One who is immersed in the consciousness of *Sri*

Vidya will be totally absorbed in the consciousness of that divine Energy and will see the entire world as the Light. We will see this light in *ashtadasa mahadwipa*—in all beings, insects, planets, in all creation.

Even an innocent, illiterate person like Kalidasa became a king among poets just by chanting the single *bijakshara, Aim.* When we recite the *Khadga Mala* daily, each and every name we pronounce assumes a form. These *shaktis* approach us, coming to us as radiant light. They surround us and reveal to us all the secrets of *Sri Vidya.* In this way, *Khadga Mala* gives us intuition and instruction in *Sri Vidya.* After being taught by these *shaktis* and light, we can then reveal *Sri Vidya* to the entire world.

Smarana or remembering the divine name

Mahā pāpa nāshini

washes away all our greatest sins, whatever they may be—all 63,000 sins that a human can commit. If one has committed a heinous crime; if a person is under the influence of a *dosha,* negativity caused by our astrological charts; if we have committed sins because of *avidya,* ignorance, or in spite of being shown the light—if we chant the *Khadga Mala Stotra* all these will be washed away.

Sri Vidya is like a vast ocean; it is used for many purposes. In ancient times, when the *rishis* practiced *Sri Vidya upasana,* they only used the *Khadga Mala* for the welfare of the world. Even ordinary people can help relieve the problems of the world by chanting this sacred *stotra.*

There is a beautiful *shloka,* the first line of which says that anytime you travel on a boat and encounter storms, when you feel helpless and anticipate a great disaster, chant this *Khadga Mala stotra* and it will control the storm.

The second line of the same *shloka* says that during war, when a lot of people lose their lives, the energy created by chanting this *shloka* travels to the place where the war is occurring and controls the violence.

When we consider the whole universe, our solar system is very tiny. There are innumerable stars and planets; innumerable galaxies put together make up this vast universe. How is it that the planets rotate with their own gravitational forces? There is a systematic way in which everything happens, a reason for all aspects of creation in the universe. *Sri Vidya says* that the *Srim bijakshara* is causing all this to happen. That is why this greatest knowledge, *Maha Vidya,* is known as *Sri Vidya.*

After learning about the glory of *Sri Vidya,* and receiving the greatest gift of the *Khadga Mala* in these classes, whoever chants this sacred *Khadga Mala* will find their life completely changed. There will be a new fragrance, energy and strength to our life because we are starting a new life with this *Khadga Mala.*

* * * * *

This morning we all had the opportunity to go to the Kanva Mukhi River, which is named after Kanva Maharshi, a great *upasaka* of *Sri Vidya.* He came to this same area where we are on retreat, and did *tapas.* In ancient times there was only forest here. There were no roads. People knew about this place even at that time. This is where the *swayambhu,* self-born, temple of Narasimha Swami, the fourth incarnation of Vishnu, appeared.

Kanva Maharshi practiced austerities for forty days here, praying for water for this region. That is why there are many ponds at the top of these mountains. During the rainy season the water collects in them, and then the river begins to flow more strongly. This river also flows in summer, but it is *antara vahini,* it flows deep within the forest at a height of almost 300-400 feet above sea level. It is not visible from where we stand now. The river bed appears to be dry, but even in the summer, the people of the nearby villages downstream get their water from it. This river exists because of the *tapas* of Sri Kanva Maharshi. Without the river, there would be no villages in the surrounding areas. There are innumerable small hamlets and little villages around this place, where people grow crops. Their only source of water is this river.

I am mentioning this because it takes effort to find the river. Only after walking a long distance, and after a hard climb, can we see the river. Just sitting here without making any effort, we cannot see the river. It has been said in the *shastras,* the sacred scriptures, that it is a *maha punya,* a great blessing, just to have a glimpse of a river. That is why, in India, when people see the Ganga River, the Kaveri River, or any other river, they do *pranamas* to the river, offering their salutations as if they had seen Mother Divine Herself!

When we were traveling in America, we saw the Columbia and the Colorado Rivers, and we offered them our *namaskaras.*[29] It is good to pay respects to rivers whenever we see them. When we went to Niagara Falls, I took some *haldi,* turmeric powder, and red *kumkum* and offered them to the waters of the mighty Falls. Most people go there simply to enjoy the beautiful scenery. But we offered the auspicious red *kumkum* and the yellow turmeric and prayed there. That is our tradition. It was really beautiful to see the rivers.

There is much we can learn from rivers. The greatest lesson rivers teach us is selflessness. Rivers supply water and give life to countless people. They provide nourishment to many insects, birds, animals, plants and human beings. They are useful in innumerable ways, yet they ask for nothing in return.

---

[29] *namaskāra:* A respectful or reverential salutation made with head bowed and the palms of the two hands folded together. It implies recognition of the *Ātman,* the divine soul, in the being who is greeted.

A river does not stop or turn back to see what is happening. It simply flows on, never losing sight of its final goal—to merge with the ocean. It never looks back. In our *sadhana*, we need to be bold and courageous like the river, always looking forward till we reach our ultimate destination, *moksha*. These are the lessons we can learn from the river.

The energy of *Sri Vidya* is there to teach us, just like the river. To reach the river; we have to walk and then climb—self-effort is needed. *Sri Vidya* is the indivisible and all-pervading energy of supreme Consciousness. It is ever-present, the source of all creation; we have to merge back into it. For the achievement of that goal, *prayatna,* effort, is essential.

Countless seekers have committed themselves to the achievement of this goal. Through their *sadhana,* with a great deal of individual effort, they finally succeeded—they attained oneness with the supreme Being. These blessed *sadhakas* glow with the blissful radiance of *Sri Vidya*. You have chosen the spiritual path and you, too, can experience that state of sublime oneness. The aim of human life is to become one with the universal Personality. Every one of you must strive earnestly to achieve that ultimate goal. Children, meditate regularly, and finally merge with supreme Consciousness, just as the river merges with the ocean.

So do not pay too much attention to the problems of life, and do not crave for the fruits of your actions. Pray for others and for yourself. When you chant the radiant *Khadga Mala,* the powerful vibration of its *mantras* will fill you with hope, energy, courage and strength. You will be able to withstand all the tribulations of this world. It will also lead you to your final destination—Self-Realization. That is the blessing *Sri Vidya* bestows on all. So do not give up your *sadhana*. Meditate regularly, and you will surely succeed!

Lokāḥ samastāḥ sukhino bhavantu 3x

* * * * *

One of the *sadhakas* has asked, "When we are reciting *Sri Lalita Sahasranama,* should the *Khadga Mala* be chanted before or after it?" The answer is: one should recite the *Khadga Mala* before *Sri Lalita Sahasranama*. Just chanting *Sri Lalita Sahasranama* is not enough. One should recite the *Khadga Mala* first, and only then proceed to *Sri Lalita Sahasranama*.

Actually, a special process has been laid down in *Sri Vidya upasana:* first the *Khadga Mala* is chanted, followed by the prayer *shlokas.* After this, the *japa* of the *mula mantra,* that is, the *Pancha Dashakshari Mantra* sacred to Devi is done. Finally, *Sri Lalita Sahasranama* is recited.

Children, as we are now entering *Sri Vidya upasana,* remember that the *Khadga Mala* is a glorious and extremely powerful *stotra*. It is very beneficial to chant it daily. Don't think, "We already have innumerable *mantras*, and now we have to do the *Khadga Mala* also!" Don't think that way.

In America, the atmosphere is quiet and serene; you can be calm and relaxed there.

Sadhaka: Amma, if we don't want to do the *Lalita Sahasranama*, can we do the *Khadga Mala Stotra* instead?

Amma: Yes. It takes only seven or eight minutes to chant the *Khadga Mala.* It is not long like *Sri Lalita Sahasranama*. Even if one is well-versed in chanting the *Lalita Sahasranama,* it still takes at least thirty minutes. Usually it takes forty-five minutes, and for a beginner, it might take fifty minutes or more. But it is very powerful.

Previously, in the Penusila Ashram, everyone chanted the *Lalita Sahasranama* three times daily—in the morning, afternoon and evening. I would take the devotees to the river, and they would chant it standing in the flowing waters. When you stand in the running water of a river early in the morning, the energy of the water current, coupled with the vibrations of the *mantras* you chant, quickly activate and energize all the *chakras* in the body. In this way, the *mantra* chants become even more powerful.

The water in the river here is only two or three feet deep, so one can sit down with the water reaching up to one's shoulders and chant the *mantras.* In America and Europe the atmosphere is very silent and peaceful. There is no noise pollution. The surroundings of residential areas are quiet and conducive to *sadhana.* When you go back home, if you have a little time, you can dedicate that time to the chanting of this powerful *Khadga Mala Stotra.* And as one of you has asked, if you do not know *Sri Lalita Sahasranama,* you can recite just the *Khadga Mala Stotra.*

There are many facets to spiritual life. Already you have learned *Sri Lalita Sahasranama, Mahishasura Mardini, Sri Suktam, Samputita Sri Suktam, Purusha Suktam* and so many *mantras!* And now you have the *Khadga Mala* added to all your *mantras!* [Laughter] But the *Khadga Mala* is very easy to memorize. You can listen to the cassette to learn the correct pronunciation of the Sanskrit words.

[Group meditation.]

Many of you have been suffering from various health problems during this retreat, but in spite of your ill-health, you have been coming to the classes to listen to the discourses, and also attending the meditation sessions. So on your behalf, and for all the devotees who are suffering with some problem or other, we have prayed every day that you become well and stay in good health.

ॐ

UNIVERSAL ENERGIES IN THE KHADGA MALA

Śrī vidyām jagatām dhātrīm śriṣṭi sthiti layeśvarīm
Namāmi lalitām nityām mahā tripura sundarīm

Yā devī sarva bhūteṣu śakti rūpeṇa samsthitā
Namastasyai namastasyai namastasyai namo namaḥ

Om hrīṅkārāsana garbhitānala śikhām
Sauḥ klīm kaḷām bibhratīm
Sauvarṇāmbara dhāriṇīm vara sudhām
Dhautām trinetrojjvalām
Vande pustaka pāśam aṅkuśa dharām
Srag bhūṣitām ujjvalām
Tvām gaurīm tripurām parātpara kaḷām
Śrī cakra sañcāriṇīm

This is the opening prayer of the *Khadga Mala Stotra.* The *Khadga Mala* is not too long—it is a short *stotra.* [Much laughter]

Om tādṛśyam khaḍgam āpnoti yena hasta
sthitena vai
Aṣṭādaśa mahādvīpā sāmrāḍ bhoktā bhaviṣyati
Āraktābhām trinetrām aruṇima vadanām
ratna tāṭaṅka ramyām
Hastāmbhojaiḥ sapāśāṅkuśa madhana dhanuḥ
sāyakair visphurantīm
Āpīnottuṅga vakṣoruha kalaśa luṭha tāra
hārojjvalāṅgīm
Dhyāyed ambhoru hastām aruṇima vasanām
īsvarīm īśvarāṇām

This is also a prayer to the Divine Mother. It is known as *dhyanam,* and it describes Devi's supremely beautiful divine form. It is chanted before the *Sri Khadga Mala namas,* names, of Devi.

Om aim hrīm śrīm aim klīm sauḥ
Om namaḥ tripura sundaryai namaḥ

This is the first name. Then we continue:

Hṛdaya devī Śiro devī Śikhā devī Kavaca devī
Netra devī Astra devī...

Here for the *anga nyasa,* and *kara nyasa,*[30] we have *Astra Devi.* We have discussed all the names up to *Astra Devi* in our classes.

Kāmeśvarī Bhagamālinī
Nityaklinne Bheruṇḍe
Vahnivāsinī Mahāvajreśvarī
Śivadūtī Tvarite Kulasundarī Nitye

These names represent the phases of the moon, from the new moon to the full moon. All the phases of the moon constantly worship Divine Mother—all nature worships Mother. The *pancha bhutas,* the five elements, worship Mother; the *shad chakras*, the six *chakras,* also worship Mother. Without Mother's light, the *shad chakras* can never bloom inside. From the day of the new moon to the day of the full moon, each day a little more light is added to the radiance of the moon. The growing light of each of these days worships Mother Divine.

"Nitye" means "the Eternal." Mother is *Maha Nitye,* the Eternal One in the form of the full moon, for it is complete.

---

[30]*aṅga nyāsa* and *kara nyāsa:* Different parts of the body are reverently touched before ritual worship. This is done to invoke the divine energies present in them.

And then follow:

Nīlapatāke Vijaye Sarvamaṅgaḷe
Jvālāmālinī Citre Mahānitye
Parameśvara parameśvarī
Mitreśamayī Saṣṭhīśamayī Uḍḍīśamayī
Caryānādhamayī Lopāmudrāmayī
Agastyamayī Kālatāpanamayī
Dharmācāryamayī Muktakeśīśvaramayī
Dīpakaḷānādhamayī Viṣṇudevamayī
Prabhākaradevamayī

Mother, You are in the form of Lord Vishnu, in the form of the Sun God—all the divinities worship You alone. All these divine energies reside in the enclosures of the *Sri Chakra,* and also in its triangles.

Tejodevamayī Manojadevamayī
Kaḷyāṇadevamayī Vāsudevamayī
Ratnadevamayī Śrī rāmānandamayī

Aṇimā siddhe Laghimā siddhe
Garimā siddhe Mahimā siddhe
Īśitva siddhe Vaśitva siddhe
Prākāmya siddhe Bhukti siddhe
Icchā siddhe Prāpti siddhe
Sarvakāma siddhe

Brāhmī Māheśvarī Kaumārī
Vaiṣṇavī Vārāhī Māhendrī
Cāmuṇḍe Mahālakṣmī

Sarvasaṅkṣobhiṇī Sarvavidrāviṇī
Sarvākarṣiṇī Sarvavaśaṅkarī
Sarvonmādhinī Sarvamahāṅkuśe
Sarvakhecarī Sarvabīje
Sarvayone Sarvatrikhaṇḍe

Trailokya mohana cakra svāminī
Prakaṭayoginī

Kāmākarṣiṇī Buddhyākarṣiṇī
Ahaṅkārākarṣiṇī
Śabdākarṣiṇī Sparśākarṣiṇī
Rūpākarṣiṇī Rasākarṣiṇī
Gandhākarṣiṇī Cittākarṣiṇī
Dhairyākarṣiṇī Smṛtyākarṣiṇī
Nāmākarṣiṇī Bījākarṣiṇī
Ātmākarṣiṇī Amṛtākarṣiṇī
Śarīrākarṣiṇī
Sarvāśā paripūraka cakra svāminī
Gupta yoginī ...

All these *mantras* are woven beautifully into a luminous garland. The names are universal energies which reside in the *Sri Chakra.* Our mind and intellect are naturally attracted to this beautiful material world. Gradually, as we chant the *mantras* in the *Khadga Mala,* our mind begins to turn inward due to the power of the *bijaksharas* in the divine names. *Mantras* such as *Maha Lakshmi*, *Varahi, Vaishnavi* and *Kameshwari* are unimaginably purifying. These are not ordinary names, they are masses of divine effulgence! All these radiant lights in the form of a divine garland, the *Khadga Mala,* enter into our body, purifying and illuminating every cell.

Whatever *sankalpa* you make, with whatever intention you chant the *Khadga Mala Stotra*—it will be fulfilled. If you wish for the solution to your problems—physical, emotional or financial—the *Khadga Mala* will be your *Kamadhenu,* the celestial wish-fulfilling cow. If you desire spiritual progress, it will make you glow with divine attributes and deepen your concentration. It will bring you whatever you want.

Or if we want the welfare of the world and make the *sankalpa,* "Let our *Khadga Mala* chant stop this war," even that will happen. Our combined *sankalpas* have the strength to bring universal peace. At present we do not have the *Khadga Mala* in English, but it will be printed soon. It is just a few pages long.[31] It is difficult to translate *mantras*. There are so many translations of *Sri Lalita Sahasranama,* but they give only the literal meanings, not the true, inner meaning. When we chant the *Lalita Sahasranama* regularly, in time the Truth is revealed to us from within. That is the secret of every *mantra*.

Suppose you chant the *Om Namah Sivaya Mantra*. Its literal meaning is, "Salutations to Lord Siva." That is the translation given in books, but we are not satisfied with that meaning. However, when we constantly chant the *Namah Sivaya Mantra* with faith and devotion, we are filled with divine light and eternal bliss within, which is far beyond any joy experienced in this world.

---

[31] *Sri Devi Khadga Mala Stotra Ratnam* with *Sri Devi Khadga Mala Namavali* is now available at the bookstore and on line at www.karunamayi.org

ॐ

THE BLESSINGS OF SRI VIDYA

Swamiji: We have been very fortunate to sit here at Amma's lotus feet to learn these words of wisdom—to learn *Sri Vidya.* The knowledge of *Sri Vidya* is hard to understand from books. It is made easy with the help of a *Guru.* Amma has been so kind to explain this great *vidya,* this *Maha Vidya* to us. She has given us new inspiration to continue to do our *sadhana* with dedication and sincerity. Our lives will be infused with a new fragrance, the fragrance of *Sri Vidya.*

Amma: Embodiments of Divine Souls, Amma's Most Beloved Children,

Like a loving mother, *Sri Vidya* teaches us to see Divinity in every living being. It tells us that everything in the world is nothing but light. It brings us a new kind of peace. *Sri Vidya* is *Atma Vidya,* knowledge of the Soul. It shows us the path of meditation. It asks us to root out our *durgunas,* the vices of impurity and negativity from our heart, and cultivate virtuous and divine qualities instead. By changing our way of thinking and filling our hearts with the fragrance of peace, *Sri Vidya* inspires us to walk courageously on the path of Truth that takes us to our ultimate destination, Self-Realization.

Sajjana sangatyam, the company of pure souls, uplifts us to a very noble and high state. In ancient times, the *rishis* sat in the forest and performed rigorous *tapas* for hundreds of years. They were very pure and holy. Once, a widow came with her only son to an *ashram* where some *rishis* lived. She began to clean the *ashram,* but in her whole life, she never approached the *rishis* or spoke to them or even came into their presence.

Her young son would fetch water from the river for the *ashram.* Many days passed in this way. The widow was not paid for her services, but she and her son used to eat the food left over after the *rishis* had eaten. It was mainly uncooked food, such as fruits, roots and herbs. Sometimes she and her son would stand at a distance and listen to the spiritual discussions of the *rishis* and the discourses they gave to their disciples.

After some time, the widow passed away. As a result of listening in to all the spiritual conversations of the sages, the young boy was able to develop *atma dhairya,* inner courage, born of the understanding of the Self. He was self-confident and courageous, and did not get overwhelmed by the loss of his mother. He did not weep; he was unmoved. The *rishis* were very happy to see his self-confidence and willpower, and gave him *mantropadesham, mantra* initiation.

Our life does not end when we are faced with bereavement and loss. No matter what problems and difficulties we face, we must never think that our life is over. Philosophy tells us that trials and tribulations come to us in life to turn us towards God. We should take our pain philosophically. One day everyone has to die; our loved ones, too, must leave their bodies. But we need to face such losses bravely, and as we are on the spiritual path, we have to grow stronger through our suffering. This was the attitude of that young boy when he was left without his mother. The *rishis* gave him *mantra* initiation, and soon afterwards, they also left their bodies and attained *kaivalya,* eternal liberation.

The boy could no longer stay alone in the *ashram,* so he left for the forest and did very austere and hard penance. When he was meditating, his heart was filled with bliss and he had a wonderful experience. He saw his heart fill with brilliant light! After a while, this experience faded, and he kept crying to see that divine light again. Pleased by his purity and devotion, Sri Maha Vishnu appeared before him and said, "Due to *sajjana sangatyam,* the time you spent in the company of the holy *rishis,* the *seva,* service, you did for them, and the discourses you heard there which enlightened you, I gave you this experience of light in this birth. You will have a much better life in your next birth, and you will attain the knowledge of *Brahman;* you will be blessed with *Brahma jnana."*

True to the words of Lord Vishnu, the boy was born as Narada Maharshi in his next life. Association with the pure sages, serving them by fetching water from the river and cleaning the premises of the *ashram,* had earned him so much merit that in his next birth he became *Brahma manas putra,* the mind-born son of Lord Brahma Himself! The word *"nira"* means "water." As he had supplied water in his previous life, he was called "Narada" in this birth. So great is the power of association with the holy ones.

Sri Vidya blesses us with the opportunity to be close to such pure and noble souls. It leads us to the vision of the all-pervasive *Brahma shakti.* We have to remove all the weeds of restlessness, *maya* and ignorance from our hearts with *sadhana.* As we meditate, our hearts will expand and be filled with the grace of Mother Divine.

Sri Vidya teaches us to see all creation as Divinity. It is not easy for us to have such a vision because there is so much negativity and unhappiness in us. Unless we meditate, we cannot rise to that level. But when we experience the light of supreme Consciousness within, we attain the highest state; we attain everything. *Sri Vidya* inspires us to reach that divine state. So we have to see God in everything—in each and every particle of creation.

What prevents us from attaining our final destination? It is nothing but the little thorns of ego and negativity that prevent our spiritual progress. They are only small hurdles.

We need to remove these thorns gradually with regular *sadhana* and burn all the curtains of ignorance. Only then can we become completely free and attain the highest state.

Let us consider a new definition of the word *rishi*. The *rishis* are not ordinary people, they are not simply pure human beings. *Rishis* are *jyoti*—they themselves are divine energy, divine light. They are *vag jyoti,* the light of speech. The *rishis* may not be visible, but we can still hear their words of eternal Truth. The statement *"Sarvam khalvidam Brahma:* Everything is verily the Absolute" is the supreme knowledge the *rishis* have given to mankind.

The *rishis* give the light of *Atma jnana,* knowledge of the Self, to those who are in the darkness of ignorance. The holy *rishis* attained this divine knowledge through their austere *tapas* of meditation.

They did not keep this knowledge to themselves; they shared it with everyone. They brought hope into the lives of suffering humanity; they inspired ordinary mortals to lead a spiritual life. They encouraged them and taught them the importance of the *tapas* of meditation. They made it possible for us to meditate. By the example of their own lives, by their teachings given in the form of many immortal *Upanishads,* they brought this sacred knowledge within our reach.

We want that knowledge, and we respect and adore the *rishis* for their *tapas*. So we need to set aside the temporary problems of life and do our *sadhana* like the *rishis*. Then we will be able to go forward in our quest for that eternal light. When we follow the path shown by the *rishis* who practiced *Sri Vidya,* this supreme *Sri Vidya,* like a loving mother, guides us and blesses us. Our hearts are gradually filled with the divine light of *Atma jnana,* supreme knowledge of the Self. In our classes here, we have been discussing the supreme light, indivisible Consciousness. In the past, we may have heard or read about *Sri Vidya*. But now, like a flash of blazing light, *Sri Vidya* has come to us and awakened us to the Truth with the inspiring words:

Sarvam khalvidam Brahma
Sarvam Shaktimayam jagat

Sri Vidya teaches us that this whole universe is glowing with the resplendent light of indivisible supreme Consciousness alone. All creation is *shaktimayam:* it is full of the energy of divine Consciousness. *Sri Vidya* has blessed us with this extraordinary, precious, joyous knowledge. Children, let the divine light of *Sri Vidya* shine brilliantly in your hearts. Worship *Sri Vidya* daily, for it has bestowed on us this supreme *vedic* knowledge which cannot be learned from ordinary human beings.

Sri Vidya brightens our life and makes it glow with the light of the true knowledge of the *Atman*. With the help of that effulgent light, we have to continue our *sadhana.* When our efforts are sincere, Divine Mother's blessings are always with us. Amma has been telling you in these classes that this great *Sri Vidya* was not revealed to the world by ordinary people. It was proclaimed by the sacred *Vedas* and also by Lord Siva Himself.

The *Vamakeshwara Tantra*[32] describes a conversation between Lord Siva and *Uma Devi,* or Parvati, His lovely consort, which took place on Mt. Kailasa, the abode of the divine couple. In this dialogue, Lord Siva reveals the secrets of *Sri Vidya* to Parvati Devi as a *prasada,* a loving offering. He was the first to speak about *Sri Vidya.* That is how we came to know about *Sri Vidya;* otherwise we

---

[32] *Vāmakeṣwara Tantra:* One of the *Tantras*. The *Tantras* are the fundamental texts of *Sanātana Dharma*. *Tantras* contain the knowledge of the various aspects of *Sri Vidyā,* including *mantra, yantra* (mystic diagram) and *kuṇḍalinī*. Their central theme is worship of the Divine as Shakti, cosmic energy.

would have known nothing about this supreme knowledge. Later, some of the *rishis* learned *Sri Vidya upasana,* and they in turn initiated a few select, deserving disciples. That is how the divine knowledge of *Sri Vidya* spread in the world.

Our classes about *Sri Vidya* will continue during the following week in the form of discussions about the great Sanskrit *stotra,* the *Saundarya Lahari.* Adi Shankaracharya composed this beautiful *stotra,* taking the essence of *Sri Lalita Sahasranama.*

Ātmavat sarva bhūtānī

is another great saying of the *Vedas,* which states clearly, "All beings are the *Atman* alone." This means that we must first realize the Divinity within us, and then we will be able to see the same all-pervading Divinity in each and every atom of the universe. The *Vedas* also say:

> *Om namo Veda vānyai namaḥ:*
> Salutations to the voice of the *Vedas*, and
>
> *Om namo Sri Vidyāyai namaḥ:*
> Salutations to *Sri Vidya.*

The *Vedas* themselves extol *Sri Vidya* as that eternal Truth which is revealed in the *Vedas.*

Without divine will and grace, you would not be here at this retreat, that is certain.We may think that we have come to this Sri Vidya Retreat due to our own efforts and planning, but behind all our efforts, the blessing of divine will and grace are essential. There are many people who really wanted to come to this retreat. They were keen to spend a few days with Amma here and learn about the wonderful subject of *Sri Vidya.* Many of them planned every detail, but at the last moment something happened and they were forced to cancel their trip. It is not that easy to come to Penusila. You have to fly from far-off countries in different parts of the world, and it is very expensive.

Actually, in every city in America, on the day of Individual Blessings, thousands of people told me, "Amma, we want to come to Penusila for the Sri Vidya Retreat." But many of them did not have regular jobs, so they could not afford the tickets. Since last year, the economy of the entire country has been bad, and people are undergoing great suffering. Even now, more than a thousand people want to come to Penusila; their hearts are here. They want to be here for this retreat and learn about *Sri Vidya,* but they have financial problems.

So all of you who are at this retreat today were able to come because of the will of Divine Mother. She made it possible for you to attend the classes and meditate here. You were able to listen to the wonderful wisdom of *Sri Vidya,* such as the *Vedic maha vakya,*[33] *"Sarvam shaktimayam:* this whole universe is filled with Shakti, divine energy," and then you meditated on that all-pervading supreme Shakti.

So far in our life, we have been concentrating our attention on ordinary thoughts and activities. But here we have been focussing on supreme energy, which is divine light, and which is known as *Sri Vidya.* This supreme Shakti alone has created all the planets, stars and galaxies. She has created the whole cosmos, and She alone pervades and energizes it. All the planets and stars are revolving in space, yet they move in a very organized manner. How does this happen? By the will of that divine Shakti only. The same divine energy which creates and controls the cosmos has brought us all together in this place to make us meditate!

---

[33] *mahā vākya*: (*mahā*: great + *vākya*: sentence) Great saying.

You all know the *Purusha Suktam,* which occurs in the *Rig Veda*. Many of you chant it daily. The ninetieth *shloka* in the tenth chapter of the fourth canto of the *Rig Veda* speaks about the grace and blessings of the Divine, of God:

Purusha evedagam sarvam
Yadbhūtam yaccha bhavyam
Utāmṛtatva syesānaḥ
Yadanne nātirohatī

Never forget this, children. Everything good and positive that we do is the result of divine grace alone. Everything good that happens in our life is also the blessing of God's grace. That is why during *homas* we chant the *Vedic mantra* which means, "May we live for a hundred years—a hundred years of good health—seeing only good things, listening only to good words, performing only good actions and always living positively." So our life must always be full of goodness, purity and positivity. And we must never give up our *sadhana*.

In the course of *sadhana,* we sometimes meet with serious obstacles and disturbances. At such times, we may give up our *sadhana*—things like this happen. Children, never stop your *sadhana* for any reason. There will always be blows and injuries in life. Divine Mother is the only one who can heal all our hurts. God alone has the power to heal our unseen wounds. Life should not come to a standstill because of the difficulties we have to face.

Live through all the trials and tribulations of life with courage. Even when you are faced with the most painful situations, take inspiration from the story of Narada and start a new life. Obstacles, problems and injuries cannot put a stop to life—it must continue. Your *sadhana* must continue.

In his previous birth, Narada was an ordinary boy who did the *seva* of fetching water for the holy *rishis*. When he lost his mother, he did not get overwhelmed with grief. He was initiated by the *rishis* and began to meditate. He had the wonderful experience of light and bliss, he had the *darshan* of Lord Vishnu, and in his next life he was born as the great sage Narada, the mind-born son of Brahma! How much spiritual evolution took place because of his sincere *seva* and meditation.

He was also blessed by *sajjana sangatya* as he was always in the company of the pure-souled *rishis*. When we always listen to good words, always see good things and spend our time in the company of spiritual people, our life is slowly transformed and a wonderful future awaits us!

Spirituality is like the pure and divine Ganga. It flows forever—it never stops. So my dear children, embodiments of divine souls, Amma's most, most beloved babies, I love you gazillions and gazillions of times. Wherever you may be, you belong to your Amma!

The time has come for us to start a new line of thought, to undertake a fresh venture, to start a new life—the great venture of a spiritual life! Let us walk on a new path in a new direction, with a new feeling and a new spirit. Let us fill our life with a new fragrance and a new light inside.

Everything in the cosmos comes from the highest Consciousness of oneness, the eternal, unmoving *Omkara*. It is absolutely silent and motionless; there is no outward sign of *chaitanya* or awareness in that *Omkara*. During the Sri Vidya Meditation Retreat, a bright ray of light has flashed out from that Consciousness, from that supreme *Chaitanya,* and touched your heart. Really, we are very blessed. My dear children, from today on, lead a spiritual life, walk the path of *dharma,* proceed with your *sadhana* and attain your highest destiny in this very birth! This is the wondrous blessing *Sri Vidya* bestows on us.

Sarvam shaktimayam jagat: Everything in this moving and changing world is supreme energy alone. You are God—you are not a sinner! The *Veda* gives us a very beautiful and elevated seat. It declares, "O man! With your breath, with your power, you purify the eight directions, plus the upward and downward directions, making a total of ten directions. With your light you illumine the sun, moon and stars. It is your energy that purifies fire!"

This is the way the *Vedas* extol man. But they add, "O man! Always have perfect purity inside; do nothing bad in this world. You have come here like a traveler, so try to help all people. Do not forget your *svadharma,* your prime duty as a human being: live in righteousness and proceed on the path of the highest spirituality, the path of *Sri Vidya,* the *sadhana* of meditation." This is stated in the *Vamakeshwara Tantra*, in the *Uma Maheshwara samvade,* the powerful dialogue between Lord Siva and Maha Parvati Devi, His divine consort.

There are sixty-four major *tantras*. All of them were expounded by Lord Siva Himself. The *Vamakeshwara Tantra* is one of the *tantras* mentioned in *tantric granthas,* the sacred *tantric* scriptures which contain the teachings of *Sri Vidya*.

Our Sri Vidya Meditation Retreat will continue with the *Saundarya Lahari*. What is meant by the name *Saundarya Lahari? "Saundarya"* means "beauty," and *"lahari"* means "wave." So *"Saundarya Lahari"* is "a great wave of beauty." This beauty is not external, it is cosmic beauty, the beauty of Divine Mother's compassionate love for Her creation. The *Saundarya Lahari* is an extremely wonderful subject, and in the opening *shloka* of this exquisite divine *stotra* Adi Shankaracharya praises Mother Divine with the words, *"Sarvam shaktimayam jagat."*

Without divine energy there is no universe. So the very essence of *Sri Vidya* is contained in the statement *"Sarvam shaktimayam jagat:* the whole cosmos, containing countless universes, is pervaded, controlled and governed by Shakti, the energy of supreme Consciousness." This supreme energy comes from Divine Mother's lotus feet. A single ray of light from Her beautiful sacred feet is enough to illumine the whole cosmos!

So where is Divine Mother? She is in the *Sri Chakra* in the *bindu sthana.* She is the central point in the innermost triangle, in the form of *Omkara.* That *bindu,* that point, is the source of the cosmic light and energy which constantly radiate from Mother Divine.

Sri Vidya is not ordinary education; it is the greatest education in this world. It is greater than all kinds of material knowledge; it is greater than all *yogas*. Lord Siva Himself says in the prayer *shloka, "Sri Vidyam jagatam dhatrim: Sri Vidya* is the mother of all creation." So *Sri Vidya* is the highest education, greater than all *yoga shastras.*

Today we are searching in every field to gain new knowledge. Man has walked on the moon, investigated Mars, and in 2005 hopes to probe Saturn! We are curious to know whether there are any living beings on other planets. But unfortunately, we have forgotten to search inside our self. What is in our hearts? If we look carefully, we will find the weeds of "I-ness, me-ness and my-ness." We forget about all the negativity inside because we are always too busy. Our life is full of commotion. We are seeking happiness in transitory, external things.

Sri Vidya gives us true awareness. Like your own mother, *Sri Vidya* comes to you and gently touches your shoulder. "Wake up, my child," She says softly, "wake up from this long dream. It is time to travel on the right path which leads to true knowledge." So, children, you need to wake up immediately. Get up before the *Brahmi muhurta,* the auspicious hour between 3:30 and 4:30 a.m. Do not sleep at that time; wake up, pray and meditate.

Kauśalyā suprajā rāma pūrva sandhyā pravartate

"O blessed son of Kaushalya, wake up! It is the auspicious hour before dawn."

Guru Visvamitra wakes up Sri Rama, the incarnation of Lord Vishnu, with these words: "O Rama, wake up! It is 3 o'clock, time to begin the day with *sandhya vandana,*[34] chanting of *Sri Gayatri Mantra* and meditation." Even Lord Rama followed this discipline.

We need awareness of our true goal, and for this, it is a special blessing that we have been able to attend this Sri Vidya Meditation Retreat. As Amma mentioned earlier, over a thousand people would have liked to be here, but were unable to come in spite of their deep desire. Children, nothing is in your hands. Everything is in the hands of the Divine. Everything happens by divine will. Surrender to divine will, and your life will become peaceful and positive. If you suffer any injuries, or problems arise in your life, that is not the end. Even death is not the end—it is only a short break, a preparation for our next life.

The *Vedas* say that we carry with us all our load of good and bad *karmas* into our next life. We are born into a good, spiritual home or a poor home according to our *karmas*. Our surroundings, our relations and friends, and all the circumstances of our life are the result of our *samskaras*. If our *samskaras* are good, we have *sajjana sangatyam,* the friendship of pure-hearted spiritual people, which gives us mental peace, contentment and a sense of fulfillment in life. We do *mantra japa, puja* and meditation in our homes.

---

[34] *sandhyā vandanā*: (*sandhyā*: the meeting point of night and day + *vandanā*: prayer) Morning or evening prayers.

So, children, have good friends. Start the day early in the morning with prayer and meditation. After meditation you can chant some *mantras* or *stotras*. Evening is the best time for chanting the *Khadga Mala*. If you want to chant the *Khadga Mala* five times, six times, or even ten times, you can do that. It is very beneficial to chant it one hundred or one thousand times. The *Khadga Mala* is a short *stotra,* and chanting it five times in the evening will not take too long as each repetition takes only seven to eight minutes.

Every name in the *Khadga Mala* is a powerful divine energy which resides eternally in the *Sri Chakra*. In the *bindu sthana* of the *Sri Chakra,* divine Consciousness, *Sri Lalita Parameshwari,* dwells in the form of the *bindu,* which is nothing but *Omkara*. When you chant the powerful *mantras* in the *Khadga Mala,* all the divine energies residing in the *Sri Chakra*—from the *bindu sthana* to the outermost enclosure—are pleased and shower their blessings on you. You get the grace of *Sri Lalita Devi* and all the *nava avarana devatas,* all the divinities residing in the nine enclosures of the *Sri Chakra.* All the Gods and Goddesses, and all the universal energies bless you when you think about them. The moment we chant a name in the *Khadga Mala,* the vibrations of that *mantra* immediately reach the divinity addressed—they touch that divine light! Such is the power of this wonderful *stotra.*

Thank you, children, for coming all the way to India for this retreat. Many of you have suffered from health problems here, and we feel sad about it. But every day we are praying for all of you, for your good health and mental peace. You are in your Mum's home, in your Mum's lap. I wish you good health, spiritual progress and liberation from all the commotion of worldly life. I love you always and always and always. I love you forever and ever, children!

APPENDIX

A MORNING OUTING WITH AMMA

(In the Ashram grounds)

Amma: That is a Ganesha tree, son. It is called *shvetarka.* It is good for people with bad tonsils.

Swamiji: This is the *arka* tree. It is born from the energy of the sun, and people worship it as the Sun God. We do not know the botanical name, but in Sanskrit it is called *arka.* It grows only in tropical countries. It has purple or white flowers. The *shvetarka,* the tree which bears white flowers, is very rare. It is worshipped as Lord Ganesha Himself because the formation of its trunk often resembles the image of Sri Ganesha. That is why, if people find it in their compounds or in some other place, they never cut it. They worship it. Sometimes it grows very big.

Its leaves have a very powerful medicinal value. They are used to treat patients with infected tonsils or mumps, which causes swelling of the neck. Fresh *arka* leaves are collected and warmed by holding them close to a charcoal fire. These warm leaves are applied to the affected area. This treatment cures many problems in the neck region.

The leaves have a lot of milk in them. When you pluck an *arka* leaf, its stem immediately begins to ooze milk. This milk is also very powerful and is used for making medicines. We have two *arka* trees in the *ashram*. We have left them where they are, and we worship them. In this region, in the surrounding areas of Nellore, we don't find the white *arka,* but the purple ones are common. White *arka* is sometimes seen in Karnataka and Bangalore.

Amma: This is *tulasi,* Lakshmi Devi.

Swamiji: Look at this pedestal which was recently built. It has eight sides, facing the eight directions. Here you will see the *ashta* Lakshmis, the eight forms of Maha Lakshmi Devi. In the limited space of just nine or ten inches, the artisans have created in cement all the forms of Lakshmi Devi! They are gloriously beautiful. All the details of their faces—their eyes, noses and lips—are clear, and all the limbs are so graceful.

Do not think that a mold was used to create these images. They have been made by hand. The artisans shaped these cement images from imagination, using only their hands, without the aid of any measurements or diagrams. The artisans are uneducated, but they are skillful artists. They have not been to school, and they know nothing about mathematics, but they can work wonders with their hands!

The *tulasi* plant is looked upon as Lakshmi Devi Herself. That is why, even today, the sacred *tulasi* is planted in front of most Indian homes and worshipped reverently every morning and evening by the housewives. Friday is considered to be especially auspicious for this *puja*.

Beside our meditation hall, between the temple and the meditation hall, there is a huge *bilva* tree. The *bilva* tree is sacred to Lord Siva. It is said that if you meditate under a *bilva* tree, its powerful and peaceful vibrations help your concentration.

In about one year, when all the new construction work is completed, the old kitchen, which has been here for twenty years, will be demolished. In its place there will be a flower garden. Then we will all be able to sit under the beautiful, sacred *bilva* tree and meditate.

Near the entrance to the *ashram* there is a *parijata* plant. It has the most beautiful, delicate blossoms, which are popularly known as coral flowers. This is because the stems of the tiny, fragile *parijata* blossoms are the color of coral. These celestial flowers come from the gardens of Indra, king of the Gods. They bloom only in moonlight, and their intoxicating scent is wonderful! The *parijata* plant was brought to the Earth from *Indra loka,* the kingdom of

Indra. Coral flowers are used for Devi worship because they are so delicate and fragrant.

Vastu of Penusila Ashram: The whole *ashram* has been constructed according to the rules laid down in *vastu shastra.*[35] The entrance to the *ashram* is from the east, according to the stipulations of *vastu.* It is auspicious to have the entrance of all buildings on the east. When we construct a large institution like this one, a college or a big factory, their entrances should be built strictly according to the stipulations of *vastu shastra.*

It is important to have the *Guru sthana,* the residence of the *Guru,* located correctly. In an *ashram,* the *Guru* is venerated and worshipped as God. The most important buildings in an *ashram,* such as the temple and the *Guru sthana,* should be placed in the southwest of the property. This is known as the *Nairuti sthana.* That is why the Bharata Mata Mandir and Amma's residence have been built on the southwestern side. Now a new meditation hall has been constructed, but the old meditation hall was in the same place.

Amma's residence has a boundary wall. According to *vastu,* it is important to have a boundary for every building. The limits of your property should be clearly defined. In the States, you don't have boundary walls for your homes. The

---

[35] *vāstu śāstra:* (*vāstu*: dwelling, site + *śāstra:* science) A revealed science concerned with the five elements and the four directions and their proper order and balance. Its purpose is to ensure auspiciousness and health to people in their dwellings and work places. In laying down rules for constructi on of buildings, for example, it takes into account the cosmic influence of the sun (its light and heat), the direction of the wind, the magnetic field of the Earth and the influence of the planets. East and North are important, for the sun rises in the east, and north is the center of the m agnetic pole.

houses are built side by side, with no demarcation lines. But just as a soul must have a body, every house must have a boundary wall. That is why we ask people to build walls around their property. If this is not permitted by law, at least plant a hedge or put up fencing and separate your land from your neighbor's. In this way the energy of all the directions will remain balanced within your own compound. If your home has been built in accordance with the rules of *vastu,* your life will be peaceful.

In the northeast corner we have a beautiful lotus pond. Amma has told us that the northeast is a good place for water; that is why the pond was made in that place. It is full of pure white lotuses. In the extreme northeast corner of the *ashram* we have a pond with pink lotuses. You must have seen them blooming there.

During this season, when we go into the interior of the forest and mountains, we see hundreds of waterfalls.

Amma: Beautiful waterfalls, *nanna.* We have some videos of these falls. There are many bees which have made big honeycombs. But it is dangerous to approach them. [Amma laughs] You have to wear a mask.

Swamiji: I have asked some people to get me a mask to protect my face.

Amma: When bees smell strangers, they get angry, *nanna.* That is why people are afraid to go near the honeycombs. Actually, Guru Vasishtha meditated in these forests. The surrounding areas are so cool and beautiful. Lakshmi, Gayatri and Vishnu Kunda are such lovely spots. Vishvamitra Muni also meditated here. We would like to take you all to see these sacred places, but the problem is that there are honeybees everywhere, and they attack strangers.

The water of the falls is very pure, like bottled mineral water. It is now *Kartika masa*[36] according to the Hindu lunar calendar. This month is sacred to Lord Siva, so it is very auspicious to bathe in the river at this time. During the month of *Kartika,* many people fast every Monday. Devotees come from Chennai and many other places, and decorate the whole Ashram with *rangoli*[37] and lights, whether I am here or not.

---

[36] *Kārtika māsa:* This month falls in November-December.

[37] *rangolī:* Colorful designs of flour, *kumkum* and turmeric powder on the pavement outside the front door of a house or building, created on festive occasions. During special *pujas* and *homas* at the Ashram, these are made in the form of sacred *yantras,* mystic geometric patterns.